Praise for Arthur Manuel and *The Reconciliation...*

"One of the most important texts on truth and reconciliation ever written. *The Reconciliation Manifesto* is a cogent step-by-step look at how Canada's colonial past created our present situation, and provides decolonizing strategies for the future . . . well-seasoned with [Manuel's] sense of humour . . . *The Reconciliation Manifesto* is an extremely valuable resource for those who are fighting for decolonization. For other readers, it may simply serve to dispel myths about Canada's colonial history. Decolonizing is a massive undertaking, and, fortunately, we've got many great Indigenous minds on the job . . . *The Reconciliation Manifesto* offer[s] strength and solidarity to Indigenous readers, and a generous guide to ally-ship for non-Indigenous readers. For the latter, these books will unsettle, but to engage in ally-ship is to commit to being unsettled — all the time."

— Carleigh Baker *The Globe and Mail*

"The late Secwepemc Nation activist's blazing final book offers an eloquent analysis of how Canada was built on a racist understanding of property and human rights. Manuel lays it all out; there's nowhere to hide. He also makes it plain that there's no reconciliation until we replace the stinking, unstable mythologies that still support the Canadian state with something more noble and true."

— Robert Everett-Green, *The Globe and Mail*

"Effectively puts the current conversation around reconciliation into the rightful context . . . Manuel is refreshingly pro-active, creative, and importantly, persuasive (not to mention witty) . . . the tone is generally hopeful . . . the writing is accessible. *The Reconciliation Manifesto* can be read as an introductory text for Canadians who have little understanding of colonialism; or, as an intervention into counter-hegemonic theorizing . . . this is nonetheless a tremendously important book for multiple audiences."

— Hayden King, *Indian & Cowboy*

"Arthur Manuel was, without question, one of Canada's strongest and most outspoken Indigenous Leaders in the defence of our Indigenous land and human rights. He travelled extensively throughout Canada, North America and around the world in his unwavering and relentless efforts to champion the cause of our Indigenous rights. He never took a step back. His legacy will continue to reverberate throughout our ongoing Indigenous history for many generations to come."

— Grand Chief Stewart Phillip,
Union of B.C. Indian Chiefs

"Art Manuel has always been among those First Nations leaders I have most admired because his take as a Defender of the Land, and as an economically switched-on person, together have propelled the First Nations case into a wider field that has proven to be vital to the propagation of their case. Like generations of First Nations activists before him, he has kept the flag flying against multiple discouragements so effectively as to have marked him a worthy son of his great father."

— Boyce Richardson, author and journalist

"Art was a true force for change. He was a powerful voice for Indigenous rights on the international scene."

— Charlie Angus, Member of Parliament,
author of *Children of the Broken Treaty*

"[Arthur Manuel] shunned violence and bitter rhetoric, for which he was dubbed Canada's 'Nelson Mandela.' It was *reductio ad absurdum*, he insisted, to portray his demands as a denial of the settlers' rights. They had built a country that was the envy of the world. They could stay. Nor did it make sense to demand 'astronomical' sums in compensation for the epidemics of smallpox, measles, influenza and tuberculosis, for the apartheid-style abuses and repression, and for the actions of officials who had aimed to rid the country of the 'weird and waning' Indian race. But Canada could treat his people justly. It could give them their fair share of profits made on their land, and above all it should drop 'discovery': the obnoxious notion that a white man, merely by sailing past a river mouth, could legally claim ownership of an empty space, as if it had no human inhabitants. "

— *The Economist*, January 28, 2017

THE
RECONCILIATION
MANIFESTO

RECOVERING THE LAND
REBUILDING THE ECONOMY

Arthur Manuel
and
Grand Chief Ronald Derrickson

Preface by NAOMI KLEIN

James Lorimer and Company Ltd., Publishers
Toronto

Dedicated to our children, grandchildren and great grandchildren yet unborn and the next generation of volunteer activists.

James Lorimer & Company Ltd., Publishers acknowledges the support of the Ontario Arts Council (OAC), an agency of the Government of Ontario, which in 2015-16 funded 1,676 individual artists and 1,125 organizations in 209 communities across Ontario for a total of $50.5 million. We acknowledge the support of the Canada Council for the Arts, which last year invested $153 million to bring the arts to Canadians throughout the country. This project has been made possible in part by the Government of Canada and with the support of the Ontario Media Development Corporation.

Cover design: Tyler Cleroux
Map sources: (page 69) Indigenous and Northern Affairs Canada, Natural Resources Canada, National Atlas of Canada; and (page 257) map created by David Carruthers, PlanLab Ltd., July 19, 2017. Map Projection: NAD 83 BC Environment Albers. Data Source: Secwepemcul'ecw Boundary, NStQ Consultation Guidelines (2009); Mining claims, BC Ministry of Energy and Mines (2016); Trans Mountain Pipeline, www.transmountain.com/map (2017); Elevation model, ESRI Canada (2017); Base map, NRCan Atlas of Canada 5M.

Library and Archives Canada Cataloguing in Publication

Manuel, Arthur, author
     Reconciliation manifesto : recovering the land, rebuilding the economy / Arthur Manuel with Grand Chief Ronald Derrickson.

Includes bibliographical references and index.
Issued in print and electronic formats.
ISBN 978-1-4594-0961-3 (softcover).--ISBN 978-1-4594-0966-8 (EPUB)

     1. Native peoples--Canada--Government relations. 2. Native peoples--Canada--Social conditions. 3. Canada--Ethnic relations. I. Derrickson, Ronald M., author II. Title.

E92.M347 2017   305.897'071   C2017-903764-1
                                             C2017-903765-X

James Lorimer & Company Ltd., Publishers
117 Peter Street, Suite 304
Toronto, ON, Canada
M5V 0M3
www.lorimer.ca

Printed and bound in Canada.

CONTENTS

Preface   9
Speech at the Funeral of Arthur Manuel
Naomi Klein

Introduction   14
Our Struggle
Grand Chief Ronald Derrickson

PART 1 GETTING TO KNOW YOU

Chapter 1   The Second Coming   48
Chapter 2   Beginning at the Beginning   57
Chapter 3   White Supremacy — The Law of the Land   62
Chapter 4   From Dispossession to Dependency   67
Chapter 5   From Dependency to Oppression   72

PART 2 THE R WORDS

Chapter 6   The Race Question   76
Chapter 7   Reserves as Holding Pens   82

PART 3 EUROPEAN LAND CLAIMS

Chapter 8   We Stole it Fair and Square   88
Chapter 9   Attempted Genocide: Political Battles
                with Pierre Trudeau   94
Chapter 10 Changing Legal and Policy Landscape —
                1984-2014   100
Chapter 11 Tsilhqot'in Case and Crown Title   109
Chapter 12 British Columbia Commission Treaty Process   113

Chapter 13   Rightful Title Holders   118

Chapter 14   Risk and Uncertainty   121

Chapter 15   Revenge of the Balance Sheet   126

PART 4 PUTTING OUR OWN HOUSE IN ORDER

Chapter 16   Neocolonialism, or Selling Our Birthright   132

Chapter 17   Where Have the Leaders Gone?   138

Chapter 18   Around the Mulberry Bush   142

Chapter 19   The Grassroots Struggle: Defenders
                 of the Land and Idle No More   150

Chapter 20   Unity Around a Strong Position   155

PART 5 THE FAMILY OF NATIONS

Chapter 21   The International Stage   160

Chapter 22   Constitutional Deadlock and the
                 International Option   165

Chapter 23   What the UN says about Self-Determination   168

Chapter 24   Canada's Human Rights Treaties   174

Chapter 25   CERD: Early Warning and Urgent Action   180

Chapter 26   International Recognition of Our
                 Proprietary Rights   185

Chapter 27   UNDRIP and the Trudeau Betrayal   191

PART 6 FALSE RECONCILIATION

Chapter 28   The Reconciliation SWAT Team   200

Chapter 29   Reconciliation Framework Agreements   204

PART 7 STANDING OUR GROUND

Chapter 30   Defending Our Land   212

Chapter 31   The Legal Billy Club   215

Chapter 32   Blockading a Mine   220

Chapter 33   Criminalization of Protest   224

Chapter 34   Non-violence, but not Passive Acceptance   229

Chapter 35   Resisting the Carbon Bomb   235

Chapter 36   Defending Mother Earth   242

Chapter 37   The Long-Term Approach   247

Chapter 38   Declaring Sovereignty on the Ground   250

Chapter 39   Standing with Standing Rock   253

Chapter 40   Death of a Warrior   259

PART 8 RE-ENVISIONING CANADA

Chapter 41   Our Inalienable Rights   265

Chapter 42   Back to the Future   269

Chapter 43   The Six-Step Program to Decolonization   275

LETTERS TO FRIENDS AND ENEMIES

1 Open Letter to Pope Francis   281

2 Open Letter to the Secretary-
General of the United Nations   283

3 Open Letter to the Queen of Canada   286

4 Open Letter to the Chief Justice
of Canada   289

5 Open Letter to the Defenders of the Land   291

Afterword
Settling with Canada: A Debt Coming Due
Grand Chief Ronald Derrickson   293

Appendix: "Are you a Canadian?"   297

About the Authors   304

Index   306

PREFACE

Speech at the Funeral of Arthur Manuel
Naomi Klein

Adams Lake Indian Band Community Centre
January 15, 2017

Many of you are here because you are related to Art through love, through blood, through kinship. Through nation to nation relationships. Some of us here are in this circle in what was referred to yesterday as the "movement family" because Art chose us. Invited us in and gave us jobs, gave us tasks. The researcher, the reporter, the lawyer, the media liaison. Art wove this amazing web of people. Some of us know each other. Many of us do not. None of us have the full picture of the web that was in Art's mind and heart and was part of the plan. And I think part of the work that we have to do to honour Art is part of what we are doing here over these days, which is to connect with each other, because Art was the glue, in so many ways. Now we have to do that work. Connect with each other and answer each others calls and emails and texts.

I became one of those people almost two decades ago, invited to be part of that journey of decolonization. Brought into this amazing community and educated by Art. Shown the beauty of the land and fed freshly caught salmon and moose meat stew — he was particularly proud about that. Brought to different protest camps, introduced to Elders and warriors, like the late great Irene Billy and Wolverine. This process was political, but it wasn't just political. It was also personal.

I spoke yesterday to Shiri Pasternak, one of the people whose lives were changed as a member of the Defenders of the Land network. She said, "Art taught us to be better people. He changed the way we saw the world. He showed us a different way to relate to the world." That was the work. It wasn't just political work. For me, what Art taught me that changed me and changed my life forever, was that what is good for Indigenous people, what will ultimately fight poverty and heal trauma, is the return of the land. And he also taught me that what is good for Indigenous people is good for the land, is good for the water, and ultimately is our only hope for fighting catastrophic climate change and ecological collapse. Our only hope. That connection between respect for Indigenous rights and the safety of all of humanity is the greatest lesson. I will carry it with me, always.

He showed us a path. He changed us. Harsha Walia said that after Art passed that she learned more from him than she did from law school. This was not uncommon. You heard about Arthur's mobile office . . . well he was also running a mobile university. And we were his students. There are so many of us. There were so many lives changed, decisions made about what to study, about what to do with one's life because of contact with Arthur.

I am so lucky to have found myself on this revolutionary road with Art. It's a road that took me to Wall Street for a meeting at Standard and Poor's where Arthur and Guujaaw, carrying writs from various Indigenous nations in B.C., met with the man whose job it was to issue Canada's credit rating and made the argument that Canada's credit rating should be downgraded from triple A to something much lower because of the unacknowledged debts owed to Indigenous peoples. This is just one example of the brilliance of Arthur's mind.

He was always looking for these pressure points. Yes he was an incredible organizer and teacher but he was also this savvy tactician. And he did things that no one had ever done. He looked at the world and he thought, okay, we are fighting these free trade agreements — I was with Art fighting the free trade agreement of the Americas in Miami and Quebec City — but he used NAFTA — even though he didn't believe in NAFTA, to intervene on the side of the Americans in a dispute with Canada. No one had ever done that before.

So he was always finding these pressure points. And he said, okay, if this is a culture that values money more than people, more than water, we will speak in that language. And we will hit them where it hurts. Using these agreements and institutions that are all about money, like NAFTA, like the World Trade Organization, we will apply this pressure. It was my privilege to witness that, to be on Wall Street with Arthur and Guujaaw. And be on the slopes of Sun Peaks and see the protest camps and see the love of the land. And to be in Bolivia with him and to have been with him so shortly before his death in Standing Rock.

Arthur Manuel was a true visionary. He had a vivid image in his mind of the way the world should be. He wasn't interested, as you all know, in cutting the best deal in this fundamentally unjust system. He wanted to change the system. He wanted to undermine the legal fictions on which the system rests.

And he knew, as we know, that that is not a job that can

be done in back rooms. It is a job that can only be done by powerful, robust, broad-based social movements using many tactics and that was the kind of movement that Art was so central to building. He was a visionary. He had the vision of the world that we need that will save us all. But he was also working on the world we have, because we are not led by political visionaries at a political level in this country.

And what that meant was that even though Art wanted to be working towards his visionary legal work and using the Canada 150 celebrations to tell a very different, unsettling story, even though he had all of these plans, he was stuck in these rearguard battles. Battles against mines that should never be built, against ski resort expansions that threatened an entire culture and way of life and, most recently, against the Kinder Morgan pipeline expansion across the waterways of this territory.

So the last months and weeks and days and hours of his life were spent strategizing and trying to figure out how to stop that pipeline. I received emails from Art the day he was hospitalized about organizing to fight the pipeline. And he was giving us tasks, organizing conferences and making plans. It was a lot that he was taking on. Too much for any one person. His son Ska7cis said, "He was always pushing all of us." So, all I can think of is maybe he has been taken from us when we need him most, when the land needs him most, when the water needs him most, when the planet needs him most, because we all need to step up and do more and dig deep for Art. When a revolutionary is taken out mid-sentence, mid-fight, the fight doesn't end. It takes flight.

A lot of my emails from Art over many years, and I have been reading them over the past days, go back a few years, a lot of them were about his wanting to write a book. Every time a book of mine would come out I would send a signed copy to Art. And he would say, one day I am going to autograph a book for you. And he did it. He did it. He wrote the book, it came out two years ago and it is magnificent.

And despite everything else he was doing, now we are finding out from Grand Chief Ronald Derrickson that he wrote another book — that there are actually two books. Which means he left us a map.

Arthur Manuel was a beautiful soul and an intellectual giant. He helped generations of organizers and theorists to understand how Indigenous land rights, if truly respected, hold tremendous power to create a more caring and generous society — and they are our only hope of protecting the planet from ecocide.

In the lives of his family and friends, Arthur's tragic death leaves a hole that can never be filled. But his unfinished work and his transformational vision will live on in the countless people he has taught and forever changed.

I wanted to leave you with words I heard from Dorothy Christian yesterday. I saw Dorothy and she said, "He left us with so much work to do."

He did. And we'll do it.

INTRODUCTION

OUR STRUGGLE

Grand Chief Ronald Derrickson

When Arthur Manuel was laid to rest on January 15, 2017, on the hillside overlooking Neskonlith, the Secwepemc community in the B.C. Interior where he was born and where he raised his own family, he was mourned by Indigenous people, friends and supporters from around the world.

In the obituaries, which appeared in the *Globe and Mail* and *The Economist* as well as in Canadian and Indigenous media across the country, he was celebrated as the main strategist of the modern Indigenous movement in Canada, by Grand Chief Stewart Phillip as a leader who "never took one step back" and by many as "the Nelson Mandela of Indigenous peoples." That was the depth and breadth of the esteem he was held in by our people. When the weekly podcast Media Indigena devoted an entire program to the theme of who could replace Arthur Manuel in the Indigenous movement, they found no one who had the stature, the political experience, the profound understanding of the issues and the impeccable character that gave Arthur such a unique place.

That is how central a role he played in our movement. It is why, immediately after we co-authored *Unsettling Canada:*

A National Wake-up Call, I told him we had to produce a second book that expanded on the ideas he developed there in a step-by-step approach, describing exactly where we are today as nations, how we arrived at this point and, most importantly, where we were heading.

This is that book. Arthur completed the final draft just weeks before his death. In these pages, you will find evidence of Arthur's brilliance as the strategist of our movement. He explains in simple, straightforward language how we, as Indigenous peoples, arrived at this place and how we can find our way out into an honourable future for our people — and especially for future generations. Along the way, he explores the ideas and the hidden struggles behind the current Indigenous resurgence, and points to a path forward for both Canada and Indigenous peoples. His piercing analysis and sharp wit cuts through the sometimes intentional fog created by those who would try to reconcile with Indigenous peoples without touching the basic colonial structures that dominate and distort our lives. No one will read this book without seeing the country differently, and without acknowledging that Arthur Manuel had a more profound understanding of how Canada actually functions — and malfunctions — than anyone of his generation.

Along with being one of the most important leaders of our generation, Arthur was my friend. Some have seen us as a kind of political odd couple: Arthur the grassroots radical, and me, better known as a businessman. Part of this perception is an oversimplification of both of us: Arthur himself had built an on-reserve business, and I served as band chief at Westbank for more than a decade fighting for the basic human, economic and Indigenous rights of my people. But it was true that Arthur tended to focus on his grassroots political vision while my focus was more on the bottom line. Any details that might have divided us were insignificant in comparison to the broad consensus we had on what needed to be done. I was happy to help fund his travels to represent Indigenous interests in New York and Geneva because Arthur was one of the most intelligent, dedicated, humble and knowledgeable leaders that I have ever known. He worked from the highest principles and he always fought for all of us.

He is enormously missed not only for his political leadership, but for his infectious laugh and sense of humour to match. He was a pleasure to be around and to head out for Chinese food with. When he told a story, and you will see in these pages that he was a master storyteller, he never belittled others and he always downplayed his own role. With his friends, and he had many of them, he was generous, thoughtful and, when necessary, protective. As a family man, a father and grandfather, he had abiding love and respect for his children and a boundless delight in his grandchildren. In all cases the affection was returned in even greater measure. Arthur Manuel was not only my most valued political confidant, but also my best friend. I miss him dearly.

Although we have been working closely together only over the past twenty years, I have known Arthur all my life — in the way our people often know each other. Arthur and I knew each other before we met, because my father was a friend of his father, George Manuel. George, a Secwepemc leader from Neskonlith, began as a local leader and ended up head of the national Indian organization and the founding president of the World Council of Indigenous Peoples. He walked with a limp from a bout of tuberculosis of the hip that had him spend much of his childhood in the Coqualeetza Indian Hospital. He had a simple, direct way of putting things, along with a quiet manner. Like Arthur, he was one of the most brilliant thinkers of his generation, and we were always happy when he would visit us as he passed through the Westbank Indian reserve. We were Okanagan and he was Secwepemc, but it was the same struggle. My family, though dirt poor, would raise money for gas for George in his political travels — with our friends and neighbours throwing what they had into the hat. I remember my father shooting a deer to sell to our Chinese friends so he could pay for a hotel room in Victoria when George went there to challenge the government on all of our behalf.

This link between our families has continued throughout my life. During my first ten years as chief at Westbank Arthur's older brother, Bobby, was Neskonlith chief, and he and I worked closely together on all of the important issues our people faced. It was through my friendship with Bobby that I became friends with Arthur.

Like Bobby, Arthur was born into the struggle. In our first book, he wrote that among his earliest memories were hearing his father, who was working with Andy Paull's clandestine political organization at the time, typing long into the night as part of his political organizing work. In the morning, his father would head off with very little sleep to his boom man job on the river. On most weekends he was on the road, travelling as cheaply as possible, sleeping in his car when there wasn't money for a hotel or in the homes of political supporters. This was the fight that Arthur would inherit from his father — and the main issue then was what was called "the land issue" and today is referred to more broadly as the decolonial struggle. But in the end it is still all about the land: who has title to it and who is the legitimate decision maker over it.

This struggle shaped his life. In *Unsettling Canada*, he described his first political action: when he realized that Indian kids in residential school were being fed worse than inmates in local jails, before the age of sixteen he organized a school strike. He never gave up the struggle.

From the beginning, Arthur was recognized for his leadership abilities. After several years of organizing native youth in Alberta, which he began as a teenager, he was elected as president of the Native Youth of Canada and led the takeover of the Indian Affairs office in Ottawa. He showed then, as he would show throughout his life, that he was fearless.

But while he was not afraid of activism in any form, he also began to understand that it alone was not enough. The fight was against a colonial government using colonial laws against Indigenous peoples and it would require a battle on many fronts. To equip himself for this more complex battle, Arthur attended law school and ended up at Osgoode in Toronto. It was there that he began to bring together his unique gifts as both an activist and a strategic thinker. Those gifts made him a powerful force, not only in the struggle against the Canadian colonial government, but internationally.

Yet at its base, Arthur's genius was always drawn from his community and the power of his own people. He returned from the east to work in community development and eventually built the gas station and store. He came to see me for advice when he was starting up his business and I followed his progress as he went on to become band chief and then to become an important national leader.

It was the rise of the B.C. treaty process and the push to terminate Aboriginal title throughout British Columbia that drew Arthur into the struggle that he would never turn back from. At the urging of his brother Bobby and an important Neskonlith Elder, Arthur ran for band chief in 1995. Shortly after his first election, he was also elected chairman of the Shuswap Nation Tribal Council. The new pressure for all B.C. bands to surrender our Aboriginal title and rights — in the same type of cash-for-land deal that the Nisga'a were negotiating — broadened and deepened the sense of alarm, and Arthur brought together all of the Interior tribes in the Interior Alliance of B.C. Indigenous Nations as a kind of joint defence organization. It was at this point that Arthur and I formed our own political alliance.

Our personal alliance and our friendship was forged, as many of the best are, in battle. In our case, the battle began in the forests of the B.C. Interior and continued all the way to the UN in New York, the US Department of Commerce in Washington and the World Trade Organization in Geneva. It was this fight that made Arthur an international leader in the Indigenous struggle and I will sketch the broad outlines of it here so you will have a sense of his political courage and his almost infallible political instincts.

As chiefs, both Arthur and I had gone separately to the Ministry of Forests and told them that it was unacceptable that our people did not have leases to log on our Aboriginal title land — which is the constitutional term for our never-surrendered territories. This was just after the 1997 landmark Supreme Court Delgamuukw decision, which recognized that Aboriginal title did, indeed, exist and that it carried with it a proprietary interest. But our federal and provincial governments don't pay much heed to the courts when it comes to recognizing the land rights of Indians and when both Arthur and I went to the forestry ministry to enquire about cutting leases for our people, the ministry official shrugged his shoulders and said, sorry guys, but all of the provincial leases had already been given out.

I told him that didn't make sense. How could we not be given logging leases on our own land while white companies — many of them American multinationals — had been stripping our lands for the past century? But the forestry official was not interested in a discussion. He was already showing me the door.

I remember driving back to the reserve with the phrase "all of the leases had been given out" stuck in my mind.

It was spoken with such finality. All of the provincial logging licences for our Aboriginal title lands had been given to non-Aboriginal companies and there was nothing we could do about it. The door had been slammed shut.

But when I reached my house, I was thinking, so what if all of the "provincial leases" had been given out? The hell with them, we don't need a provincial lease. We'll go log with an Indigenous licence.

That is exactly what I did. I first went to my Council and received strong support from Mike De Guevara, Chad Paul and Mick Worstik. I then went to the Okanagan Nation Alliance, our tribal council, and asked them for an Indigenous permit to log on Aboriginal title Okanagan lands. After staring at me blank-faced for a moment — because these permits had not yet been invented — they understood and the chairman of the tribal council issued Westbank First Nation a permit to log on Okanagan Aboriginal title lands.

It is hard to exaggerate the shock that we caused when we set up our logging operation without a provincial permit. The Ministry of Forests was down on us in a moment demanding we cease and desist without their permission. When we told them we had a permit, an Okanagan Indian permit, we got that same blank expression. And then a look of contempt. It was not legal under their imposed system and they would force us to quit. They would chase us back onto our reserves as they had always done in the past.

That was to be expected from government. They were in the business of stealing our land and stealing our logs. But what was surprising, although probably shouldn't have been, was the reaction among many Indigenous groups. They did not jump onto our bandwagon. They were not slapping us on the back for standing up or lining up behind us for support, but instead were looking worriedly from the sidelines, like people do in Hollywood movies when two gunslingers show up on Main Street. They looked for a place to hide. After being beaten down for a hundred years, many of our own people were frightened by our act of defiance. This was understandable. Our people were poor and clinging to what little they had, concerned that anything that upset the order of things, even the oppressive order they faced, would threaten their survival. This feeling was even more apparent among many of the entrenched leaders who made their careers by selling our peoples' subservience to the government in exchange for their own highly paid jobs and generous funding for their organizations. It was this group, who I refer to as "hang around the fort Indians," who had the most to lose and were the first to begin scurrying for cover. They would not be on our side.

I was feeling very lonely in my defiance when suddenly the phone rang. It was the familiar and very welcome voice of Arthur Manuel. He told me that he had just heard that I was in a standoff with the provincial government over logging. I told them that we were and that we didn't have many allies. Arthur didn't hesitate.

"We'll back you 100 per cent," he said. "Neskonlith, the Shuswap Tribal Council and the Interior Alliance."

These were, at the time, the organizations he was heading in his fight against the land surrender deals the government was trying to force on the Interior peoples, so I knew his words had considerable weight.

The next day he was in my office with his legal councillor, Wayne Haimila, reviewing how the Shuswap Nation Tribal Council and the Interior Alliance could support our Indigenous logging venture. I knew Arthur's support would immediately strengthen my hand in my discussions with the provincial government and we decided at that meeting that we would also threaten to organize an international boycott of B.C. forestry products unless the government backed off and freed up forestry leases not only for Westbank, but for every single band in British Columbia.

When I made that threat public the following day, the impact was massive and immediate. Newspaper editorials from across the province attacked us as B.C. job killers and, within hours, I received a call from the office of the provincial forestry minister, David Zirnhelt, requesting a meeting. I had hoped that they were getting ready to negotiate a fair deal with us, but instead the minister tried to bully us. He was going to draw a line in the forest. If Indians wanted cutting rights, he told me, the bands were free to bid at the forestry auctions with the entrenched forestry companies, both domestic and foreign multinationals. There would be no Indian leases. No concessions.

I walked out of that meeting and told the press who were waiting at the door, "All he offered was for us to pay for the trees we already own. The international boycott is on."

Arthur had already lined up the Interior Alliance to support us, putting all of its resources into shutting down B.C. forests if the ministry refused to allow Indigenous people from taking logs off their Aboriginal title lands. Arthur, who was a firm believer in deeds being more important than words, also announced his Neskonlith people were joining us — they would be heading out to log on a Shuswap Tribal Council permit.

After we had succeeded in spreading alarm through the forestry industry and among the British Columbia political elite, Arthur and I met to discuss how, exactly, we were going to launch the international boycott. It was then that we realized that neither of us had a clue about how to pull it off. We didn't have contact with the groups either inside or especially outside of Canada who could give such a boycott teeth. But it was typical of Arthur that he was unfazed by this. He followed the way of our fathers and grandfathers that insisted if you could not find a path through the woods, you made one yourself. That conviction would lead him, over the next several years, into an alliance with American environmentalists and then to the financial capitals and the power centres of the world as he fought for the recognition of our Aboriginal title and rights and our proprietary interest in our own forests.

When we discussed this, we determined that he had to start by founding a new organization, which eventually became the Indigenous Network on Economies and Trade

(INET), to pursue the issue beyond Canada's borders. That struggle was detailed in *Unsettling Canada* and eventually resulted in three of INET's *amicus curiae* briefs being accepted by the World Trade Organization and one by the North American Free Trade Agreement, showing how Canada's failure to recognize and compensate Aboriginal people for the lumber taken off their traditional lands was a form of subsidy to the lumber industry.

Arthur was helped in this by young Austrian activist Nicole Schabus, who had just completed her law degree with a special interest in human rights. She had envisioned a life of writing lofty UN human rights submissions when she met Arthur on one of his lobbying trips in Europe and, as Arthur had an ability to do, he soon enlisted her and her special expertise into the legal briefs he was working on. In fact, Nicole completely rewrote the drafts and I remember Arthur mentioning that a white person with a Canadian education could not have done what she did, because for almost all white Canadians at the time the fact that "Indians" still had ownership of this land was unthinkable. Nicole's help was invaluable then and continued to be as she became not only his partner in activism but also in life.

In the end, the WTO and NAFTA rulings set important precedents for Aboriginal title and rights in Canada. And he went further, bringing our case again and again to the United Nations in New York, where he would go on to serve as the co-chair of the international Indigenous caucus of the UN's Permanent Forum on Indigenous Issues.

Arthur was also a member of the board of directors of the Seventh Generation Fund for Indigenous Peoples and a spokesperson for the Defenders of the Land, an activist network aligned with the Idle No More movement.

But again, he knew that the fight for rights could not only be focused on the courts or international organizations. They had to be claimed directly on the ground at the community level. And so he went on to back the direct action protests against the Sun Peaks resort development on Secwepemc lands even when it was met by fierce resistance from the government, the developers and the surrounding communities. He was, indeed, as Grand Chief Stewart Phillip said about him, the leader "who never took a single step back."

Arthur's refusal to take a step back put him at odds with our more establishment political organizations, which for many years now have made a habit of walking back on our principles, so he was increasingly drawn to movement politics with a significant emphasis on international work.

This period also began his most fruitful one as the leading strategic thinker for the movement. He developed the theory of colonialism as the interplay of dispossession, dependency and oppression and he situated the battle once again on the land question. In *Unsettling Canada: A National Wake-up Call*, he set out the issues with his characteristic directness:

> It is the loss of our land that has been the precise cause of our impoverishment. Indigenous lands today account for only 0.36 per cent of British Columbian territory. The settler share is the remaining 99.64 per cent. In Canada overall the percentage is even worse, with Indigenous peoples controlling only 0.2 per cent of the land and the settlers

99.8 per cent. With this distribution of the
land, you don't have to have a doctorate in
economics to understand who will be poor
and who will be rich.

Only weeks before his death he expanded on this theme
in Russell Diabo's *Strategic Bulletin*:

Our impoverishment is a big part of the crippling oppression Indigenous Peoples suffer
under the existing Canadian colonial system.
This 0.2 per cent systemic impoverishment
is used as a weapon by Canada to keep us
too poor and weak to fight back. It is used to
bribe and co-opt Indigenous leadership into
becoming neo-colonial partners to treat the
symptoms of poverty on the Indian reserve
without addressing the root cause of the
problem, which is the dispossession of all of
the Indigenous Peoples' territory by Canada
and the provinces.

Fortunately, though, we have this book, where Arthur
sets out his vision, distilling the sometimes complex ideas
behind the current Indigenous resurgence in a single work
that can be read by both Indigenous and non-Indigenous
people who are willing to look at the real problems and find
real solutions.

You will see that Arthur is especially critical of the big
"L" and small "l" liberals who are trying to divert from the
real issues — the land question and the right of Indigenous
nations to self-determination — into a question of programs
and services. As he put it:

What is almost always lacking in addressing the issue of Indigenous peoples in
Canada are the facts. When politicians like
Justin Trudeau speak about Indigenous
peoples, they invariably use relationship language, like they are discussing a
failed marriage. They offer mea culpas for
Canada's past behaviour and call for reconciliation, as if all we needed was a bit of
counselling, an "honest conversation" so
we could find out how things went astray
between us and then, finally, we could
forget the past and head into the future
together hand in hand.
But these are not simply behaviour questions
where if Canada is nice, everything will be
fine. The issue is not behaviours but
fundamental rights — our land rights and
the inalienable right to self-determination.
The remedy is not apologies and hugs but
recognition and restitution.

Canada, he says, cannot solve its Indian problem with
measures "that are designed — as they always have been
since the first missionaries arrived, through the whole residential school experience and in the fitful Liberal bursts into
nothingness like the Kelowna accord — to fix Indigenous
peoples. This will never succeed because we are not broken.
Canada is the sick one in the relationship, suffering from
what sometimes seems like an incurable case of colonialism.
It needs to change profoundly."

For Indigenous activists, this book is also something of a warning shot — suggesting that if Indigenous people do not come together to demand their liberty soon, they will lose it. Today, victory is possible and even in sight — but it is far from guaranteed. After *Unsettling Canada: A National Wake-up Call*, this book is Arthur's call to action. Now it is his final call, but the reverberations of his words will continue to be heard and to inspire action for many years to come.

Many are listening. There are many others who identify with the warrior wing of the movement who are determined to push ahead on the ground with the change he called for. This could be seen during his three-day wake in his community when activists and warriors from across the country came to pay their respects. Several times, when the coffin was open for public viewing, they circled it and with fists in the air, chanting traditional songs and fight songs from the American Indian Movement. Reminding us that for many in Defenders of the Land and Idle No More, Arthur Manuel was not only one of the main strategists of the movement, he was their war chief.

For these, this book provides both a battle map and precise reasons that this battle must be fought. For the less engaged reader, it provides the basic facts of history that are too often distorted or simply denied.

What follows between these pages is Arthur Manuel's testament. It is laid out as he wrote it, with each section examining the large themes facing us and short chapters exploring the thematic implications in some detail.

In *Unsettling Canada* I wrote that what gave me hope in our movement were not only the brilliant thinkers and activists like Arthur, but the explosion of creativity from our artists that emerged with Idle No More. My daughter Kelly, a singer/songwriter, responded to the tragic news of Arthur's death by suggesting we work on a tribute song to him — one that describes his character and sums up Arthur's impact on our lives:

> Patient is the man
> and strong are his words
> to fight without fighting
> never yells to be heard
> Teaching Our People, humble and grace
> This is my friend, I could never replace

Arthur's passing has left a deep hole in our hearts, but it is comforting to know that his children, and my children, and this whole new remarkable generation of activists and artists that are following in our footsteps, will carry forward his torch for freedom and justice for all of our people. The torch he passed on was burning bright, and this book lights the way.

Arthur Manuel first went to the United Nations in Geneva, Switzerland in 1999 to attend the Working Group on Indigenous Populations (WGIP). There he met Chairperson Erica-Irene Daes and invited her to attend the Protecting Knowledge Conference in February 2000 in Vancouver. She is pictured with Arthur at the Conference during a briefing alongside Mi'kmaq Kji-keptin Alex Denny (background right) and Prof. Russel Barsh (background centre).

In April 2001, the Summit of the Americas was hosted in Quebec City where contentious negotiations were undertaken on the proposed Free Trade Area of the Americas. Arthur mounted a campaign to "Stop Free Trade with Indigenous Property" and attended the mobilization in Quebec City after the area was tear-gassed. He is pictured here with other activists.

Secwepemc Elders decided to oppose the proposed major expansion of Sun Peaks Resort in the mountain area known as Skwelkwek'welt. As the Chief of the Neskonlith Indian Band, Arthur supported this decision made by his Elders and women, and attended an April 2001 demonstration alongside Russell Diabo (centre) at Sun Peaks.

In mid-2001, as Indigenous leaders were killed and disappeared in Colombia for protecting their land, Arthur joined a Minga human rights mission. He attended an Indigenous mobilization in Cauca, Colombia and addressed over 30,000 Indigenous community members in attendance.

During the continuing Sun Peaks protests, a number of Skwelkwek'welt Protection Centres were set up, only to be removed by the police and the resort. Arthur is pictured here with community organizer Janice Billy at a camp set up at McGillivray Lake in late 2001.

In April 2002, Arthur and Nicole Schabus (pictured here in front of the United Nations), travelled to Geneva. They lobbied the World Trade Organization (WTO) which had just accepted the *amicus curiae* brief by the Interior Alliance Nations, setting out that the non-recognition of Indigenous land rights constituted a subsidy. They met with all the parties and third parties in the softwood lumber dispute case before the WTO.

In 2006, Arthur attended the World Social Forum in Caracas, Venezuela. He travelled with Mayan spiritual leader Lix Lopez (far right), who had already worked with his father George Manuel at the World Council of Indigenous Peoples (WCIP). They met with former WCIP Vice President Noeli Pocaterra (centre left), then Vice President of Venezuelan Parliament, and Bolivian Indigenous member of parliament Julia Ramos.

Arthur and Nicole Schabus attended the Conference of the Parties to the Convention on Biological Diversity (CBD), in Curitiba, Brazil in March 2006, fighting for Indigenous prior informed consent. During the trip, Arthur and Nicole travelled to Iguazu Falls, an area of high biodiversity.

Arthur travelled to Kenya in late 2006 and again in 2007 for the World Social Forum in Nairobi. He is pictured here meeting with a Maasai women's collective producing traditional beadwork.

As part of the lobby against unsustainable logging practices in his territory, Arthur travelled to the Weyerhaeuser headquarters in Washington State in April 2007 to make a presentation. He is pictured here with Brant Olson of Rainforest Action Network and Tara Scurr of Amnesty International.

Arthur attended many marches protesting, for example, violence against Indigenous women, pipelines and climate change. He is pictured here in August 2007 during a march at Hastings and Main, Vancouver, the poorest postal code in Canada. Arthur would often go there to "check on his people."

In 2007, Arthur did an extensive speaking tour through Australia, including a large conference in Sydney. He is pictured here in the outback on his drive from Alice Springs to Darwin, where he spoke at Charles Darwin University.

Arthur attended every session of the UN Permanent Forum on Indigenous Issues (UNPFII), where he often co-chaired the North American and global Indigenous caucuses. He helped many Indigenous peoples to be heard, including Laura Calmwind from Kitchenuhmaykoosib Inninuwug, who attended in 2008 to decry the jailing of her chief and counsel for opposition to the proposed Platinex mine in their territory.

Arthur led the Indigenous opposition to the 2010 Olympic Games in Vancouver, making submissions to the International Olympic Committee as early as 2002, opposing the candidacy and coining the slogan "No Olympics on Stolen Indian Land" which thousands yelled during the protests. He is pictured here at the Olympic Tent Village with activist Harsha Walia (right) in February 2010.

As a member of the board of the Seventh Generation Fund, Arthur travelled internationally in support of other Indigenous peoples. He is pictured here at an Indigenous mobilization in Quito, Ecuador in June 2010, alongside fellow board member and former President of the Confederation of Indigenous Nationalities of Ecuador, Luis Macas (left).

Arthur had Indigenous friends and family around the world and when they visited he took them on "revolutionary road trips." In this July 2010 photo, Arthur took Justyce and Fiona Coe, visiting from Koorie territories in Australia, to see Nez Perce Chief Joseph's grave on the Colville Reservation in Washington State.

The Conference of the Parties to the Convention on Biological Diversity (CBD) in 2010 took place in Japan, where the Nagoya Protocol on Access and Benefit-sharing was finalized, including provisions on Indigenous prior informed consent. Arthur and Nicole Schabus, pictured here at the Itsukushima Shrine, took this opportunity to visit Hiroshima.

Arthur with all his living children and grandchildren in late 2011, after the passing of his son Neskie. Pictured here are his daughters Kanahus, Mayuk and Snutetkwe; his son Ska7cis with daughter-in-law Nathalie; grandsons Aaron, Mahekan, Sqalecw, Ske7cissiselt and Pexmes; and granddaughters Suli, Mallinali and Anaoni. Arthur deeply loved his children and grandchildren and did not want them to have to fight the same fight.

Arthur served as board member and treasurer of the Seventh Generation Fund, the longest-standing and largest Indigenous foundation south of the Medicine Line. He attended the bi-annual Keeping the Homefires Burning conferences, including in 2012 in Santa Ana Pueblo, New Mexico. Pictured here at that conference, from left to right: Tupac Enrique Acosta, Arthur, Tonya Gonnella Frichner, Henrietta Mann, Tia Oros Peters, Oren Lyons, Ray Williams and Chris Peters.

In 2012, the Indigenous Network on Economies and Trade co-hosted the International Seminar on the Doctrine of Discovery. During the conference, Arthur took fellow presenter Walter Echo-Hawk (left) to visit to the Kamloops Indian Residential School, which Arthur attended.

Arthur worked closely with Indigenous rights support groups in Europe, including in Germany, France, Switzerland and Austria. He was a honourary member of the Working Group for North American Indians (AKIN), pictured here at a meeting in Vienna in 2013.

Grand Chief Ronald Derrickson sponsored and co-hosted the Aboriginal Title: Value It! Conference in May 2014 with the Indigenous Network on Economies and Trade. Some of the presenters included, pictured from left to right: Ryan Day, Yulia Kalenikova, Elmer Ghostkeeper, Pam Baley, Joan Kuyek, Russell Diabo, Grand Chief Stewart Phillip, Shiri Pasternak, Bertha Williams, Emma Feltes, Arthur, June McCue and Nicole Schabus.

Arthur was one of the founding members of Defenders of the Land, a group that brings together Indigenous activists from across Canada. Pictured here is a meeting in Mi'kmaq territory in May 2014.

Arthur with his daughter Kanahus and Grand Chief Ronald Derrickson at their May 2015 book launch for *Unsettling Canada* at the Vancouver Public Library. Arthur spoke to hundreds of Canadians at similar book launches in Toronto (together with Naomi Klein), across the prairies, throughout British Columbia and internationally.

Arthur often attended meetings of UN human rights bodies to show how Canada's policies and laws violate Indigenous and human rights. He is pictured here participating in the UN Human Rights Committee hearing on Canada in July 2015 in Geneva.

In late summer of 1995, shortly after Arthur had become chief, the Gustafsen Lake stand-off took place. Armed forces moved in just days after Dudley George was killed at Ipperwash, and fired over 77,000 rounds and used land mines. Here, in 2015 at the twentieth anniversary of the stand-off, Arthur stands with the Ts'peten Land Defenders, including Elders Wolverine and Flo Sampson.

Arthur encouraged Indigenous leaders to work together with academics to address difficult questions regarding Indigenous territorial governance. He was a co-applicant for the Determining Access project, which brought together Indigenous leadership from the B.C. Interior and academics from across Canada. He is pictured here at the Determining Access conference in February 2016 alongside Chief Russell Myers Ross (left) and Prof. Kent McNeil (right).

Arthur travelled to Geneva in May 2016 to present an Early Warning and Urgent Action submission to the UN Committee on the Elimination of Racial Discrimination (CERD). He is pictured here in conversation with UN CERD members, including then CERD President Francisco Cali Tzay (far right), the first Indigenous President elected to this position.

Arthur attended the Congress of the Humanities and Social Sciences in Calgary in May 2016, where he spoke on a panel about the Determining Access project. He was also presented with the Canadian Historical Association's Aboriginal History Prize for Best Book for *Unsettling Canada*. He is pictured here with Naomi Klein (left) and Cindy Blackstock (right) before Klein's Big Thinking lecture.

Arthur would often take his family on houseboat trips on the Shuswap Lakes, so they could better understand the way their ancestors travelled through the territory by canoe. On board this time in September 2016 were his daughter Snutetkwe, niece Anissa, most of his grandchildren including baby Wasayke, his Austrian in-laws Erich and Traude, Nicole Schabus and family friend Lix Lopez. He loved the name of the boat and kept asking "Where's my Cheque?" for the use of my land and waters.

The camp at Standing Rock hosted thousands and became one of the largest Indigenous mobilizations ever, in this case against the Dakota Access pipeline. Arthur travelled to the camp twice, in September and December 2016, with the Seventh Generation Fund. He also visited his daughter Kanahus and his grandchildren who lived there for three months.

Arthur went on his first international trip when he was 21. He travelled to Mexico and spent time in Peto in the Mayan heartland of Yucatán, at a farm that had been bought back to benefit Indigenous peoples. Forty-four years later, in 2016, he travelled back to Peto and again visited Chichen Itza, the Mayan sacred site, remarking on the impacts of mass tourism there and the dispossession of Mayan peoples, especially on the so-called Mayan Riviera.

All images are from Arthur Manuel's personal photo archive, courtesy of Nicole Schabus. Photographed or provided by Nicole Schabus except: UN 2002 by Olivier de Marcellus; Caracas 2006 courtesy of Noeli Pocaterra; UNPFII 2008 by Gawan Maringer; Ecuador 2010 courtesy of the Seventh Generation Fund; Value It! 2014 courtesy of the Aboriginal Title: Value It! Conference; Defenders of the Land 2014 by Corvin Russell; book launch 2015 by Chris Albinati; UN July 2015 by Peter McFarlane; CERD May 2016 by Peter McFarlane; and Standing Rock 2016 by Tupac Acosta.

PART 1
GETTING TO KNOW YOU

CHAPTER 1
THE SECOND COMING

Today, as Indigenous peoples, we confront our greatest hopes and our greatest fears.

We see a new and very public openness in Canada toward us and our rights, and lofty talk of reconciliation and a shared path into the future. But in the shadows behind the scenes, the negotiations to force us to surrender our Aboriginal title to our lands continue apace. In fact, they may even be accelerating.

Yet hope remains, even if it comes with caution. In the week leading up to the release of the landmark Truth and Reconciliation Report, which revealed the devastating effects of the forced incarceration of our children in residential schools on our peoples and cultures, the chief justice of the Supreme Court of Canada spoke the previously banished G-word. On May 28, 2015, Chief Justice Beverley McLachlin admitted that Canada had attempted to commit "cultural genocide" against Indigenous peoples in its residential school system that was quite openly designed to "destroy the Indian in the child."

The Truth and Reconciliation Report had been six years in the making. The three commissioners heard more than

6,750 survivor and witness statements from across the country, covering over a century of abuse at Indian residential schools. The report made ninety-four calls to action, including sweeping ones like adopting the recommendations of the 1996 Royal Commission on Aboriginal Peoples, which itself had more than four hundred recommendations. It also called for the adoption of the United Nations Declaration of the Rights of Indigenous Peoples (UNDRIP), as well as numerous recommendations that the government dramatically increase its social funding to Indigenous peoples.

In what seemed astounding at the time, the leader of the then-third party in the House of Commons, Justin Trudeau, promised to enact every one of the report's ninety-four calls to action, even though they also included items not within the government of Canada's control, like a papal apology to Indigenous peoples.

When Trudeau swept into power in the fall of 2015, with a notable number of Indigenous MPs and a renewal of his promise to at long last make right Canada's dealings with the Indigenous peoples, there was something very close to elation in many sectors of Indian country — especially in those sectors that could reasonably expect the win to result in personal financial gain, as well as political support.

Hopes were raised even further when the government released Prime Minister Trudeau's mandate letter to the new Minister for Indigenous and Northern Affairs, Carolyn Bennett. She was told that her "overarching goal will be to renew the relationship between Canada and Indigenous Peoples" on a "nation-to-nation relationship, based on recognition, rights, respect, co-operation, and partnership." The letter then provides a programs and services checklist of "issues most important to First Nations, the Métis Nation, and Inuit communities — issues like housing, employment, health and mental health care, community safety and policing, child welfare, and education."

And of course she would be expected to "support the work of reconciliation, and continue the necessary process of truth telling and healing, work with provinces and territories, and with First Nations, the Métis Nation, and Inuit, to implement recommendations of the Truth and Reconciliation Commission, starting with the implementation of the United Nations Declaration on the Rights of Indigenous Peoples." Finally, the letter promised "an inquiry into murdered and missing Indigenous women and girls in Canada."

With hardly a moment to catch our breath, the prime minister was selecting the Indigenous leadership he wanted to work with and whisking them off to Paris for the climate change talks. Virtually all of these leaders were already directly or indirectly in the pay of the federal government and when photos were taken on the plane with the prime minister, they could not contain their joy. Not only because they were being taken to Paris, but because they believed that at long last they were being taken seriously. They were going to the conference not just with Canada's prime minister but with all of the most important leaders of the world. While they posed for selfies on the plane, they were being assured by the prime minister's advisors that they would, indeed, be taken seriously.

But there was no time to reflect. At the world conference, Prime Minister Trudeau was front and centre, proclaiming that Canada was back, meaning the Canada that had enthusiastically signed the Kyoto protocol — before the Harper regime reversed Canada's position — was now at the table again and ready to not only endorse but lead the climate change bandwagon. And they did. While the climate progressives fought to have a 2 degree increase in temperature as the absolute highest rate, Canada urged that the world do better with an astounding 1.5 degree cap. By all accounts there was euphoria on the Canadian team, including the Indigenous representatives who felt they had been part of a moral crusade to lead the world back to sanity.

I was also hopeful at the news out of Paris, but at the same time, something was bothering me, although I couldn't identify exactly what it was.

It was the next day I remembered that indeed, the previous Liberal government had trumpeted the Kyoto accord and the Minister of Environment had even named his dog Kyoto. They had enthusiastically accepted the Kyoto targets but then . . . nothing. They had done nothing, absolutely nothing toward actually reaching them. That was why, when the Conservatives had come to power in 2006, it had been so easy to dismiss Kyoto. It was gone with the wave of a hand because there was no framework or even a vague Liberal plan in place to actually implement the dramatic measures that would be required to meet the Kyoto targets. In their rush to Paris, the Trudeau Liberals hadn't bothered to change the anemic targets the Harper government had set. Even after championing the 1.5 per cent goal in Paris, the Liberals did nothing to change Harper's wholly inadequate targets.

But there was little time for reflection. In December 2015, again the new Trudeau government and Indigenous peoples held a number of important symbolic meetings designed to set the tone for the next four years. The first encounter was Justin Trudeau's address to the Assembly of First Nations (AFN) in Ottawa.

The AFN national chief, Perry Bellegarde, made a ceremonial entry with the prime minister. I was not at the event, but I did see it on the news. What struck me most was the behaviour of the national chief. During the entry ceremony he was obviously very happy to be with the prime minister. Too happy, perhaps. The ceremonial dance Perry was dancing alongside the prime minister was not the controlled rhythmic walking to the drumbeat of a leader, but the bouncy young person's dance. This worried me.

I became even more worried when the prime minister said he would carry out discussions on a nation-to-nation basis, and he was clearly referring to discussions with Perry and the AFN.

The AFN is not a "nation." It is a lobby group that is funded almost 100 per cent by the government. Perry was dancing with joy because, essentially, he was dancing for his boss — the man who pays his salary.

We are told this is a time of great hope. But for those who are fighting for our rights as Indigenous peoples, it is also a time of great worry.

In the twentieth century the Liberals were in power for sixty-nine years and they adopted the assimilationist 1969 White Paper policy, which the Conservatives then picked up and continued. The White Paper was drafted by Justin's father, which also spoke in glowing and ambitious terms about justice for Indigenous peoples — when what they really meant was our disappearance by absorption into the melting pot. I knew this from personal experience because my own father, George Manuel, was put up by Indigenous peoples in Canada to fight against it and they did, finally, pressure Pierre Trudeau to withdraw it.

So I must admit I was a little more suspicious than most when again, out of the blue, Canada announced that it was officially adopting the UN Declaration of the Rights of Indigenous Peoples — a document that they had fiercely lobbied against before it was enacted by the UN General Assembly on September 13, 2007. And then Canada was one of only four countries in the world — along with the US, Australia and New Zealand — to actually vote against it. When the US administration of Barak Obama agreed, finally, to adhere to its principles in 2010, Canada also agreed to accept it, but only as an inspirational document, whatever that meant. But now, here it was, the Trudeau government Indian Affairs minister standing at the podium at the United Nations in New York and not only endorsing the UN Declaration of the Rights of Indigenous Peoples, but truly, it seemed, embracing it. Cheers went up. UNDRIP was, after all, a virtual declaration of independence for Indigenous peoples. Among its important provisions are guarantees for our right to our own nationality, which belongs to "an indigenous community or nation, in accordance with the traditions and customs of the community or nation concerned."

UNDRIP calls for the cessation of violence against us, "including forcibly removing children of the group to another group." It demands our protection from "any action which has the aim or effect of dispossessing us of our lands, territories or resources." It says states must provide restitution "with respect to their cultural, intellectual, religious and spiritual property taken without their free, prior and informed consent or in violation of their laws, traditions and customs."

UNDRIP clearly states that "Indigenous peoples have the right to establish and control their educational systems and institutions providing education in their own languages." It declares: "States shall consult and cooper- ate in good faith with the indigenous peoples concerned through their own representative institutions in order to obtain their free, prior and informed consent before adopting and implementing legislative or administrative measures that may affect them."

UNDRIP is unequivocal on the land question: "Indigenous peoples have the right to the lands, territories and resources which they have traditionally owned, occupied or otherwise used or acquired" and "Indigenous peoples have the right to own, use, develop and control the lands, territories and resources that they possess by reason of traditional owner- ship or other traditional occupation or use." It also states, "Indigenous peoples have the right to the conservation and protection of the environment and the productive capacity of their lands or territories and resources."

And perhaps most important of all, UNDRIP is unambig- uous on our fundamental right to self-determination, which is denied in a thousand ways by the Canadian government, in every syllable of the *Indian Act* that still is used to control our lives. In Article 3, UNDRIP states: "Indigenous peoples have the right to self-determination. By virtue of that right they freely determine their political status and freely pursue their economic, social and cultural development."

It seems that our future was set. In UNDRIP, the government had recognized our right to self-determination, to keep our Aboriginal title lands, which constitute the over- whelming majority of Canadian territory, and negotiate only on the use of them — deciding under the formula of "free, prior and informed consent" what development or resource extraction could and could not take place there. We were heading, finally, to our singing tomorrows.

But wait.

What was this?

Immediately after the UNDRIP adoption, the Liberal natural resources minister, Jim Carr, announced that the Liberal government is in the process of developing a "Canadian definition" of UNDRIP. Carr did not say how this Canadian definition would be implemented or whether it would be contained in possible legislation on UNDRIP and its application to federal laws. A few weeks later, the other shoe dropped. Justice Minister Jody Wilson-Raybould made the government's new stance on UNDRIP perfectly clear to a meeting of the Assembly of First Nations by saying that, finally, it was impossible to adopt it into Canadian law. This is what she said when she tossed aside the most important advance in Indigenous rights in the past five hundred years of history:

> Simplistic approaches such as adopting the
> United Nations declaration as being Canadian
> law are unworkable and, respectfully, a politi-
> cal distraction to undertaking the hard work
> actually required to implement it back home
> in communities.

So there it was. A sleight of hand. The Liberals had not in fact adopted UNDRIP, the one passed by the UN General Assembly in 2007, it had adopted some undefined Canadian version of UNDRIP whose actual content they would decide behind closed doors and, finally, the declaration would apparently change nothing in Canada because it was designed to conform to existing Canadian laws and policies. This was, indeed, another Kyoto, publicly adopting it with passion and then immediately killing it by emptying it of all meaning. All that was left was for Jody to call her dog Undrip and the parallels would be complete.

Under this government, what we'll be left with will be a few budget measures to, in the words of AFN Chief Perry Bellegarde, close the gap. They will be measures that are designed — as they always have been since the first missionaries arrived and through the residential school experience and the fitful Liberal bursts into nothingness like the Kelowna accord — to fix Indigenous peoples.

This will never succeed because we are not broken. Canada is the sick one in the relationship, suffering from what sometimes seems like an incurable case of colonialism. It needs to change profoundly. And we must work with every fibre of our being to ensure that Canada does change.

I refuse to give up. Despite the profound disappointment by many Indigenous people in the Trudeau second coming, I still see hope, a faint light on the horizon. This is the gradual dawning of awareness among ordinary Canadians that things are not right and things have to change, that there may be important projects in protecting the land and fixing Canada to make it a land of justice for all. Even if this government may well be fraudulent, now is the time to appeal to our brothers and sisters in Canada to join with us in demanding justice from a country that has often trumpeted it, but rarely delivered.

Many Canadians want to see reconciliation between the settlers and Indigenous peoples. But that cannot be forced. Reconciliation has to pass first through truth. And we still have not had enough of that from this government or from Canada as a whole. This book is an attempt to provide the truth that comes before reconciliation. And then try to plot where that new path may lead us.

CHAPTER 2
BEGINNING
AT THE BEGINNING

What is almost always lacking in addressing the issue of Indigenous peoples in Canada are the facts. When politicians like Justin Trudeau speak about Indigenous peoples they invariably use relationship language, like they are discussing a failed marriage. They offer mea culpas for Canada's past behaviour and call for reconciliation, as if all we needed was a bit of counselling, an "honest conversation" so we could find out how things went astray between us and then, finally, we could forget the past and head into the future together hand in hand.

But these are not simply behaviour questions where if Canada is nice, everything will be fine. What is broken is Canada and the issue is not merely behaviours, but fundamental rights — our land rights and the inalienable right to self-determination. The remedy is not apologies and hugs but recognition and restitution.

So let us together look at the facts of our relationship. I will not go into great detail here but it is important that as people of good faith, we take a moment to unravel our twisted histories together. Only then can we can begin on that long and complex process of fixing what is so obviously broken.

For that we must begin at the beginning. I will not dwell on our distant histories, but for those non-Indigenous who wish to understand us, it is important first to understand how differently we see the world.

In your histories, which we were all forced to learn in your schools, you paint portraits of intrepid explorers and swashbuckling privateers, men, always men, of courage and resourcefulness conquering the world for the honour and privilege of their kindly kings and queens. Beautiful fairy tales.

But when we read these histories, we do not see noble explorers. We see invaders, thieves, marauders, enslavers and rapists.

Sorry. But that is what we see and that is what the evidence shows.

If you go just a little further back in your history, you will see this as well. You will see that the assault on our land and our peoples was no romantic crusade or accident of history — it was a premeditated crime. It was not a few bad apples, it was a wave of legalized pillage and plunder that landed on our shores. In fact, the legal roots of the assault began before the Europeans knew we existed or we knew they existed, and the target was Africa.

The most brutal aspects of colonialism were launched by an Italian scholar, Tommaso Parentucelli, who was elected pope in 1447, taking the name Nicholas V.

On June 18, 1452, Pope Nicholas V issued the papal bull *Dum Diversas*, legitimizing the slave trade. That legal charter gave European kings "full and free permission to invade, search out, capture, and subjugate the Saracens and pagans and any other unbelievers and enemies of Christ wherever they may be . . . and to reduce their persons into perpetual servitude."

Three years later, the Pope broadened the licence from stealing people to stealing lands and goods as well, and expanded it to include all Christian kings. He authorized European Christian states "to invade, search out, capture, vanquish, and subdue all Saracens and pagans . . . and the kingdoms, dukedoms, principalities, dominions, possessions, and all movable and immovable goods whatsoever held and possessed by them and to reduce their persons to perpetual slavery, and to convert them to his and their use and profit."

Europe had issued a declaration of war on the world with the unleashing of an unprecedented wave of terror.

That is where our history begins. If we want to begin a process of reconciliation, this is where we have to start.

On Turtle Island, as in Africa and other peaceful regions of the world, your European forefathers first inflicted sheer terror. You do not have to read very far to see the breathtaking cruelty of Christopher Columbus and the early conquistadors and the brutality of many of the early settlers who offered money for our scalps or undertook germ warfare against our people. In Canada, the same ferocity of Pope Nicholas V's "explorers" resulted in the extermination, the complete genocide, of the Beothuk people in Newfoundland because, it was said, they were pilfering European fishing supplies that had been abandoned on the shore over the winter.

This is our despair. But we can also see a flicker of light when we look back because this initial assault was not the end of the story. There was another chapter when a new source of wealth swept through the ever-enriched Europe, and Europeans suddenly realized they needed our skills in a lucrative new business, the fur trade. We discovered that, depending on the economic climate, Europeans could change from one approach to the other on a dime. This was the case when wealth became fixed on furs to keep the new European bourgeois warm in the winter and this required a partnership with our people. Europeans had neither the technology nor the skill to hunt the furs — or even to travel through our lands — without our help, so they had to make deals with our Indigenous nations.

This partnership lasted almost two hundred years and it is during this period that the possibility of living side by side and respecting one another seemed to be a real possibility. But finally it was only a function of the business environment at the time. Once that changed, the marauders returned.

In the 1800s when the fur trade waned and was replaced by the lumber trade, Europe, after destroying its forests, needed a new source of wood and our lands were singled out. This meant lumbermen, mills and immigration into large swaths of our land. They began, finally, to devour our country. Stripping the forests, scraping away at the mineral wealth and finally, on the prairies, butchering the buffalo into extinction to make room for their own European starvelings to settle on our lands to farm in what they would call the "breadbasket" of their empire.

It was, in most of our territories, incremental theft. By gradually moving and expanding onto our lands, feeding us a steady diet of falsehoods and fraudulent deals, they took advantage of the peaceable nature of our societies and our natural North American willingness to interact with others until they were able to build up their numbers to swamp us, and gradually the trading posts morphed into military posts and we found ourselves a people under occupation.

Equally pernicious as these attacks on our peoples was the determination to write us out of existence, to remove all record of our self-governing existence in the country's founding document, the *British North American (BNA) Act*. This was, in fact, the true genius of Canada — legalizing and even normalizing genocide and the grand theft of half a continent in their founding document.

CHAPTER 3

WHITE SUPREMACY — THE LAW OF THE LAND

I do not fault the average Canadian for their ignorance because the very basis of Canada's relations with Indigenous peoples has been wrapped in falsehoods. The most blatant of these was repeated by Prime Minister Harper during the 2009 G20 meeting in Pittsburgh when he stated, without any irony, that Canada "has no history of colonialism. We have all of the things that many people admire about the great powers but none of the things that threaten or bother them."

What was most shocking about these remarks was not so much that they were a funhouse mirror of reality but that many, perhaps even most Canadians would agree with them.

Canada, as a society, is still in denial about their historical and current colonialism when it comes to Indigenous peoples, and how their country is still largely based on the white supremacism of their founding document, the *British North American (BNA) Act*. Colonialism is not a "behaviour" that can be superficially changed by a prime minister professing "sunny ways." It is the foundational system in Canada.

Canada was created by an Act of British parliament in 1867. It was more a corporate reorganization, a hurried consolidation of debts, than the birth of a nation. The problem was that they were using the theft of our lands, tucked into what, for them, was this innocuous-sounding Section 91.24 of the *BNA Act* to cover their debts.

This was where Britain, the colonial power, gave the young successor state the exclusive control of our lands and peoples. In the infamous Section 91 of the *British North America Act*, which sets out the long list of federal responsibilities, Subsection 24 lists "Indians and land reserved for Indians." That's it. That's where the whole ugly weight of colonialism is compressed, the black hole that devoured our land and liberty, where the Canadian state claims the privilege of exercising 100 per cent control over Aboriginal and treaty land and Indigenous peoples. It is where the Canadian state fulfilled Pope Nicholas V's exhortation in a more modern setting to "vanquish, and subdue all Saracens and pagans" and confiscate "all movable and immovable goods whatsoever held and possessed by them and to reduce their persons to perpetual slavery."

It is where it is most clear that the *BNA Act* was a white supremacist document designed for a white supremacist country. I know, calling Canada a white supremacist country sounds controversial to some, but it shouldn't. Blacks and Asians were systematically excluded from Canada until well after the Second World War and the few allowed in were here for very specific reasons — cheap and expendable labour to build the transcontinental railway in the case of the Chinese and as domestics or railway porters in the case of Blacks. The overwhelming number of jobs were simply refused them and the numbers of what are now called visible minorities were kept, by strict immigration rules, to less than 1 per cent of the total and very intentionally white population. For Indigenous peoples, the goal was to manage us into what was thought our inevitable extinction while their towns were kept clear of us by Jim Crow laws and practices that were in effect across the country, in some places well into the 1960s.

But the real focus of Canadian racism at its founding was usurping Indigenous peoples. Less than ten years after Canada was formed with the merger of Ontario, Quebec, New Brunswick and Nova Scotia, the young state adopted the *Indian Act*, the most colonial piece of legislation imaginable for dominating and controlling every aspect of the lives of the "subject nations" within its territories. Our peoples were to be administrated by bureaucrats in the Indian Affairs branch, generally headed by a military man. Less than ten years after the *Indian Act* was passed, the Canadian successor state was sending troops to the West to attack our peoples and seize our lands, if necessary to starve us into submission, as part of the sea unto sea mission of this new aggressive imperialist state. The very fact that the *Indian Act* is very much in force today, 150 years after Confederation, is an indication of just how deeply this colonial ideology is imbedded in the Canadian psyche, as well as into its legal framework. The two are inextricable and they will be until Canada comes to terms with its past and sits down with Indigenous peoples to define a new future together.

By the time the forces of Anglo-Canadian Imperialism were ready to move into British Columbia in the early 1800s, Canadians were so certain that they had broken our people that they did not even bother with formal treaties. They simply pushed us aside and when groups like the Tsilhqot'in resisted, they lured their leaders out of their camps and executed them.

Everywhere they imposed the colonial reserve system and *Indian Act* dominance to exercise their dominion over us. Dispossession was the goal and dispossession was complete. Canada was and remains a thoroughly colonial country, built on the dominance of one race over another for the purpose of seizing and occupying their land.

In some places, like British Columbia, Canada began as an apartheid state. I know even the most sympathetic Canadian is raising their eyebrows when I compare Canada to the former apartheid state in South Africa. But in fact, the first act of the new Crown colony in British Columbia in 1872 was to pass a bill forbidding Indigenous peoples from voting. The reason? At the time, Indigenous peoples outnumbered the non-Indigenous population by four to one in the province as a whole, and fifteen to one in places like the north coast. This was to be a race-based democracy and racism would be the main, and quite explicit, guide to governance until the whites greatly outnumbered the Indigenous peoples. It is as if the South Africans had managed to make apartheid unnecessary by swamping the blacks by white immigration. That is exactly what the white society in British Columbia did and, at different times and in different ways, what all of Canada did. The underlying apartheid is still there. And that is why I say that Canada will remain a racist society until it comes to honourable terms with the Indigenous peoples of the land. This is what has to be fixed in Canada.

The phrase in the *British North American Act*, "Indians and land reserved for Indians," gave the new Canadian government complete power over our lands and peoples.

In these words, Canadians see only a bureaucratic line in their British-made Constitution. But to understand what you have done, I ask you to substitute the names of other peoples. Would you not be outraged by a founding state document that asserted the government's absolute control and domination of "Jews and land reserved for Jews" or of "Negroes and land reserved for Negroes," when it also clearly stated that Jews and blacks were not considered "persons" under the law and had no democratic rights within the society? That they were excluded from citizenship and were refused even the right to vote?

Contained within this Constitution were Canada's equivalent of the 1935 Nuremberg laws, Canada's equivalent of Jim Crow in the American South. That is how serious our fight is against the white supremacy packed into section 91.24 of Canada's founding document.

You cannot simply reform your racist state by enacting a few more programs and delivering a few more services. It is imbedded in the very nature of Canada and requires a completely new deal, which I will discuss later. But first, to truly understand where we have landed today, we have to continue retracing a bit further along the sad road that brought us to this place.

CHAPTER 4

FROM DISPOSSESSION TO DEPENDENCY

It began with our dispossession: our lands were stolen out from underneath us.

The next step in the colonial process was to ensure that we were made dependent on the interlopers so they could control every aspect of our lives. They had to strip us of our ability to provide for ourselves. This was done by cutting us off from access to our land. My father, in his book *The Fourth World*, wrote how this was achieved in the B.C. Interior by literally fencing us off from our lands. Suddenly, our hunting grounds, our fishing spots, our berry patches and other gathering places were cut off by fences and then enforced by a maze of regulations, while our timber was carted away and our lands stripped of our minerals. This had never even been envisioned by our people. Even when we allowed the newcomers to set up settlements on our land, it was unthinkable that suddenly our lands would be closed to us.

We were suddenly corralled onto reserves under the authority of an Indian agent and given a few gardening tools for sustenance. In some areas, where the land was particularly fertile and the Indigenous peoples managed to generate small surpluses and tried to sell them, local white farmers complained about the competition and laws were passed forbidding us from selling our produce.

Even today I find this with my own community. The Secwepemc warrior, Wolverine (William Jones Ignace), who recently passed away, was an important Elder in our nation. As an old man he single-handedly ran an eight-acre organic farm and gave his produce away to the needy in the community. But he was not allowed to sell it at the local non-Indigenous controlled farmers' market. It is important to note that our poverty is not a by-product of our domination but an essential element of it.

But of course, it was not easy to keep us off our land. In my grandparents' time, there was no welfare. Our people still survived by fishing, hunting, picking berries and working seasonally as farm labour, as ranch hands or in the woods. We had to find ways to make money all year round and to gather a significant portion of our food from our lands surrounding the reserve.

Welfare was introduced on the reserve quite late and again its main purpose seemed to be to keep us corralled on our reserves.

When it was first introduced, people were actually reluctant to take it. The Indian agent came and said the government was going to give us "relief money" and our people were instantly suspicious.

There was a big debate on the reserve about whether we should accept it or not. People tried to understand why the white man would offer to give us this and no one could figure it out. That was when I was young. People were always trying to figure out what the white man was thinking and we never could. It was always a very delicate situation with the white man.

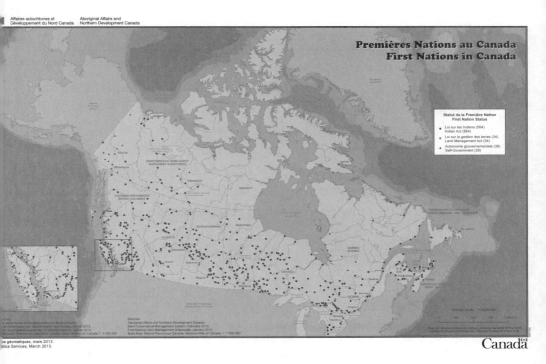

Indian reserves account for just 0.2 per cent of our territory. Canada claims 99.8 per cent of our land.

You would listen to what they said, but what they said often made no sense at all. I remember people coming to see my father to ask if they should take the relief money. Because he worked on the river for the lumber company, my father had more contact with the white man, so people would always ask him what he thought of those things.

He told them that if they needed it, they should take it. The logic was that it was due to us because they had fenced off our lands from us and pushed us up against the river on the tiny reserve. But for my father, it was never more than a stopgap measure. He devoted his life to trying to get back our land and our right to govern ourselves.

In the immediate term, welfare cheques would play an important pacification role. It meant our people spent less time on our land and it allowed the white man to bring in all sorts of laws forbidding us from hunting and fishing and trapping on our territories.

When these measures were put in place, the Canada we see today was finally created. Indigenous peoples, from enjoying 100 per cent of the landmass, were reduced by the settlers to a tiny patchwork of reserves that consisted of only 0.2 per cent of the landmass of Canada — the territory of our existing reserves — with the settlers claiming 99.8 per cent for themselves.

Looking at it in another way, while Indigenous peoples are around 5 per cent of the population, we have been left with just two tenths of 1 per cent of the 100 per cent lands that were originally given to us by our Creator. This is, in simple acreage, the biggest land theft in the history of mankind. This massive land dispossession and resultant dependency is not only a humiliation and an instant impoverishment, it has devastated our social, political, economic, cultural and spiritual life. We continue to pay for it every day in grinding poverty, broken social relations and too often in life-ending despair.

But that was always part of the plan. We were left isolated and hungry while our land generated fabulous revenues from the lumber, minerals, oil and gas and agricultural produce. We were to be kept penned in on our 0.2 per cent reserves until we were starved out and drifted into the skid row in the city and gradually disappeared as peoples.

Our dependency was not some accident of history. It is at the heart of the colonial system. Our poverty is not an accident, the result of our incompetence or bad luck, it is intentional and systematic. The brilliance of the Canadian system as it has evolved is that today our poverty and misery is actually administered by our own people. In the spirit of what seems to me as profoundly insulting, this system is even called by some "self-government." Self-government as designed by the Canadian government is a system where we administer our own poverty.

The dependency built into this system can be heartbreaking. I once even heard a young person on the reserve saying that she could not wait until she was eligible to receive her own welfare cheques. That is how bleak their future is. That is all they had to hope for in life. Their own welfare cheque. That is what colonialism leads to: complete and utter dependency. When this is the best they can hope for, it is not surprising that the suicide rate among our young is among the highest in the world.

And please do not tell me that you can solve this with a new program or new services administered from Ottawa or by Ottawa's agents in our communities. Or by giving us hugs or tearing up when you speak of our misery. There is only one program to solve this dependency and despair, and that is to get rid of the deadening weight of the colonialism that causes it. For us to once again have access to our land and for the settlers to recognize at last our Creator-given title to it.

But again I am getting ahead of myself. There are a few more stops to make on this tour through a past that I know you, my non-Indigenous readers, would like to forget. But once again it is important to look at what has been broken if we hope to put the pieces back together.

CHAPTER 5

FROM DEPENDENCY TO OPPRESSION

The final element of the triad of colonialism, after dispossession and dependency, is oppression.

Indigenous and Northern Affairs Canada (formerly Department of Indian Affairs) was created to manage our dependency until we either died out or were assimilated into the settler culture and our Aboriginal and treaty rights extinguished.

What we know is that if we resist golf courses being built over our ancient cemeteries as was the case in Oka, the eviction from our sacred sites and ceremonial places as was the case at Gustafsen Lake, the building of ski resorts on our land as in Skwelkwek'welt, or fracking oil and gas like in Elsipogtog, we are confronted by the RCMP or provincial police paramilitaries or even the Canadian army. That is what colonialism is in Canada.

Indigenous peoples who try to defend their land are met with swift repression and land defenders are overwhelmed by military or paramilitary forces and carted off to jail.

This is despite the fact that the Supreme Court of Canada has already addressed the matter of our Aboriginal title and rights in a number of historic rulings and our fathers' and mothers' generation successfully fought to get recognition of Aboriginal title inserted in the *Canadian Constitution Act, 1982*, as we will see in later chapters. But the Canadian government has time and again acted outside the law, refusing to implement our Supreme Court recognized Aboriginal title and rights on the ground. The Canadian government instead holds firmly to its colonialist principles and its colonial past.

This is easy to understand. The Canadian settlers seized our land under section 91.24 of the *British North America Act, 1867* and the provinces entered onto our lands under section 92, under which provincial authorities claim the right to licence the cutting down of our trees, allocating our lands to the settlers and the digging of mines and damming of our rivers. The wealth and economy of Canada and the provinces is based on this colonial Constitution that dispossesses Indigenous peoples of their land and makes us dependent on the federal and provincial governments. When we try to assert our rights, Canada and the provinces use the courts and the police to sweep us aside. For Indigenous people in Canada, the colonial law enforcer meets us at every turn. It is still common, even with our court acknowledged Aboriginal and treaty rights, for Indigenous peoples who are caught hunting and fishing off their tiny Indian reserves to be arrested and their fish and game taken from them. If we try to keep resource extractors from moving onto our lands, injunctions against us are quickly awarded and the police swoop in for mass arrests. Canadian jails are full of our young men and women. That is colonialism. That is oppression. One breeds the other.

It is also important to note that colonialism has been condemned by the United Nations in all its manifestations because it is against world peace. It is against world peace because once you dispossess and make dependent a people you automatically create the yearning to be independent and free. This will always result in the human struggle for human freedom and independence. We will also look at the implications of this in greater depth later.

PART 2
THE R WORDS

CHAPTER 6
THE RACE QUESTION

I know Canadians, even many of those who support us, are a bit tired of hearing about racism. I am sorry and I will keep this section short, but this issue has to be aired once again, if only for you to understand what a wounding weapon you wield against us — against Indigenous men and women, and more importantly against Indigenous children.

For Indigenous peoples, racism is the invisible force that fills the jails and too often the graves with our people in a way that also ensures a minimum resistance at the community level. Racism is one of the essential tools of colonialism and without understanding the workings and effects of racism, you cannot fully understand Canadian colonialism.

I say it is essential because how can you condone the seizing of a continent by one race from another if not by theory of racial superiority. Indigenous peoples have to be portrayed as lesser beings for natural law to allow them being swept aside. Without racism, you cannot justify your history. So in a real sense your history is based on racism.

Racism is both your justification for your right to seize our land and a sharp-edged tool you use to break the body and spirit of our people, to try to ensure that all of us, from our children to our Elders, wake up in the morning with the feeling of being useless, worthless, helpless, in fact "less" in every way than white Canadians, and it tells us that our condition is our fault. Because of this, we undervalue not only ourselves and our communities but, importantly, even the value of our land. Racism is the silent and often hidden weapon that Canada uses against us, and exposing it is the only way to combat it, to bring it out into the open and force Canadians to deal with it. It is at the same time a devastating weapon and a debilitating mental illness that you must cure yourself from if you hope to see the world as it is and begin to make the healthy choices that you must make for your own, as well as our, survival.

It has been there from the beginning. It was the ugly face of racism that allowed the British fishermen who came to Newfoundland in the seventeenth and eighteenth centuries to methodically and mercilessly exterminate the Beothuk people. In the twenty-first century, it is the face of Canada that, sitting across from us at the government negotiating tables in Holiday Inn meeting rooms, demands we terminate our existence as peoples. It is the force behind the murder and disappearance of hundreds of our women and behind the police refusal to properly investigate what has and still is happening to them.

Racism is central to Canada's relationship with Indigenous peoples. As noted, it plays the dual role of both justifying the theft of our lands and as a cudgel to beat us down so we cannot rise up to seize them back. This, finally, is the evil heart of Canada we are fighting against. What we are fighting for is our land and our dignity — and the two are inseparably intertwined in the anti-racism and anti-colonial struggle.

RACISM: FACTS AND FIGURES

If you want to measure the effect of Canada's racist and colonial policies toward Indigenous peoples you only have to look at the fact that while Canada was recently number one in the international quality of life indicator, Indigenous peoples within its borders languished at number seventy-eight.

When you apply the United Nations Human Development Index to Indigenous peoples they are way down at level seventy-eight, and Canada is at level one. These figures are from a few years ago, but the pattern is consistent year after year. So when you put people on 0.2 per cent of their territory, you literally generate a system of impoverishment within that community. Indigenous peoples have always fought against that.

Canadian racism drives us into and keeps us in third world conditions in Canada. Here is the story of our lives in numbers.

On-reserve Indigenous people are more than six times more likely to be on social assistance than non-Indigenous people but the welfare amounts are dramatically less than non-Indigenous people, at $168 a month. An amount of money that in no way can sustain a healthy and dignified human life.

At the same time, three times as many of our people live in houses requiring major repair and we are six times as likely to live in over-crowded houses. And each year while gradual improvements are made for non-Indigenous housing, ours continues to deteriorate. We are far behind and we are still losing ground.

It is no surprise then that being born Indigenous in Canada means that you will live an average of nine years less than non-Indigenous people. That in itself is a shameful fact. In something as fundamental and precious as life itself, Indigenous people in Canada are given a short shrift.

And it starts with our youth, who are more than three times as likely to live in poverty and more than ten times as likely to be taken away from their families. Indigenous people are less than half as likely to get a high school education and if they do continue, the government will spend a third less on their schooling as it does on non-Indigenous children.

Suicide rates among Indigenous youth are five to six times the national average, as is their incarceration rate. Among Indigenous women, this incarceration rate is eight times the national average. And incarceration rates for both Indigenous men and women are rising every year. Canada has apologized for forcing generations of Indigenous peoples into the soul- and culture-destroying residential schools but in reality it has only substituted jails for the schools in the forced institutionalization of our peoples.

That is the racism we live with on a day-to-day basis. If you are still not convinced, I suggest you read the 2015 *Maclean's* article, "Canada's Race Problem? It's Even Worse than America's," which compared the situation of Indigenous peoples in Canada with the situation of black people in the US and found, to their great surprise, that by every metric from unemployment through to life expectancy, Indigenous peoples in Canada fared far worse that blacks in the US to the point where even *Maclean's* was forced to admit that "by almost every measurable indicator, the Aboriginal population in Canada is treated worse and lives with more hardship than the African-American population . . . Unfortunately, the truth is we have a far worse race problem than the United States."

This is the shameful face of Canada that Canada tries to hide from the world. This is something we must expose every day, forcing Canada to look at itself in the mirror. Then we must address real solutions to the issue of Canadian racism, which begin and end with the land issue.

When they stole our land they stole our past and our future and they made us into figures of contempt, beggars on our own land. The fight for our land is our fight against racism and a fight to reclaim our past and future.

COLONIALISM = RACISM

Under the present Canadian system our dependence and our poverty are almost total. Suffering this impoverishment is even more painful when we are forced to watch the settlers who live on our land enjoy almost 100 per cent of our natural wealth and resources. Colonialism in Canada means we either live in poverty or we assimilate and disappear completely into the settler society. Colonialism in Canada is cultural genocide hidden behind the notion that Canadians are smart and civilized and Indigenous peoples are stupid and primitive.

The real cause of our profound distress is, of course, that we do not have power over any land or resources in our Aboriginal and treaty territory except for the 0.2 per cent of our territories that has been designated Indian reserve lands. We have no access to our own Aboriginal and treaty lands to build a sustainable economy for our people, so we always look stupid and primitive. The settlers who have access and control over 99.8 per cent of our territory always look smart and civilized.

The ugliest thing about the settler-Indigenous relationship is that Canada secretly looks at our poverty as a final step toward our ultimate extinction as a peoples.

The real problem with this kind of colonial relation-ship is that it does not even consider the human toll on the lives of the Indigenous peoples. It is like Harper said in Pittsburgh in 2009: "We have no history of colonialism." You can see in this glaringly dishonest assessment of Canada that Indigenous peoples do not even measure up as human beings. Indigenous peoples are merely "nothing" in his assessment. We are on our way to oblivion because Canada will not give up the near total power and control they have over Aboriginal and treaty lands. And once again, this is not a matter of Indigenous peoples being collateral damage in the colonial system. Our oblivion is precisely its objective.

CHAPTER 7

RESERVES AS HOLDING PENS

Poor people corralled on reserves, who are dispossessed of their wealth, are much easier to control. When they react in anger and despair, the only people they have to lash out at are each other. At that point, the criminal justice system comes into play and our people are carted off to jail. That is the Canadian solution. To build as many prisons as it takes to control our young men and, increasingly, our young women. And this serves the system perfectly well.

After the dispossession of our territories, leaving us with 0.2 per cent of our land and the settlers with 99.8 per cent of our land, the reserve system itself was constructed as a series of holding pens for the assimilation of our peoples.

Proof that reserves were set up as such can be seen in the fact that reserves cannot, like every other community in Canada, grow with the needs of the community for space, but are tiny fixed points where any population increase adds to impoverishment and where unsustainable increases are finally forced off the land and the territory to be submerged in the city — too often in skid row. This is a point that is too often overlooked. Imagine the situation in Toronto in 2017 if the city was forced to keep the exact same boundaries

it had at its incorporation in 1834 — east to west from the
Don Valley Parkway to Dufferin and north to Bloor, or
roughly 3 per cent of the territory of Metropolitan Toronto
today, not including the hundreds of square kilometres of
suburban sprawl that surrounds it. If Toronto had been an
Indian reserve in 1834, the community's inhabitants would
be forever limited to that tiny postage stamp of land and its
residents would not have been permitted to construct even a
shed outside of those boundaries during all of this time. That
is entirely the situation with Indian reserves in Canada. Our
communities can never ever grow. Excess population must
leave and abandon our way of life. The severe overcrowding
on our reserves reflects how deeply our people are committed
to our way of life. The fact that Canada tries to strangle us on
our reserves shows how deep their contempt is for us.

Canada has intentionally given us no room to breathe
because Canada's Indian policy has always been based on
strangling us until our cultural and economic lives were
destroyed and we have been irrevocably forced from our
lands and assimilated into their cities as, at best, small ethnic
groups in their multicultural mosaics. The obvious reason
is that if we can be made to disappear as peoples, the land,
finally, will be theirs alone.

Even in recent years, my family has experienced this. It
was one of those illuminating moments when we were told,
point blank, what Canadians wanted from us.

The people of my community, mainly youth and
Elders, were occupying the part of our territory known as
Skwelkwek'welt, where the Japanese company Nipon Cable
moved in not only to upgrade a small ski hill operation but to
install a complete resort town in the mountains with twenty
thousand hotel and condo beds on wilderness lands we used

for hunting and gathering wild fruits, vegetables and medicines. The development was carried out at a breakneck pace to get it installed before the protests could expand to meet it and the Japanese company was aided by a bizarre land grant from the provincial government that increased the amount of Secwepemc land available to them at the same pace they developed it. The province also passed a special law to give that multinational development company the status of a municipality, which meant it controlled all zoning issues and even law enforcement on its territory. All this they were doing on our Aboriginal title lands.

Our land defenders built camps to protest this theft and exploitation without our permission. Police were sent up to arrest our people en masse. After the first round of bitter confrontations, mass arrests were made. Then all of the charges were suddenly dropped. We thought that perhaps the company and the police had seen the light, that they were prepared to negotiate with us. When the police came to confirm to us that, yes indeed, the charges were being dropped, one of our leaders and my good friend, Janice Billy, said, "Fine, can we go back up there now?"

The police said, "No."

Janice asked, "Where are we supposed to go then?"

The police shrugged. "Just stay on the Indian reserve."

All of the arrests, the harassment and the clubbing our people had taken at the hands of the police now made perfect sense. That is what they wanted from us. Stay on our 0.2 per cent Indian reserves and leave the 99.8 per cent stolen lands to the foreign business interests. That was the only thing that would save us from police repression — because that was the purpose the repression. To keep us walled in on the tiny postage stamp sized lands allotted to us.

Our people went back up to Skwelkwek'welt to reclaim our land. The police swooped back in with more beatings and arrests. This time the charges were not dropped. Among those jailed were my own daughters. The bulldozers swept all aside and the police jailed those who had dared defy them. That was the penalty for our people stepping off the reserve without permission. That is the reality in modern Canada.

And after the arrests are made and the brief press coverage is forgotten, we are left with the consequences. My daughter Mandy was in jail, separated from her infant son. With other family members, I helped look after him and brought him to her each week in the Vancouver jail. I saw her heart break each time that I would have to leave with her child and the haunted look that you could see even in the photos of the day of her release.

I write this because the human dimension is important in these struggles. Indigenous and environmental activists suffer and their pain is very real. In his book, *The Fourth World*, my father wrote that when he was working on the river, a white co-worker came up and asked him, in all seriousness, if Indians had feelings. We certainly do. It is because we have deep feelings for our people and for justice that we struggle in the first place. At the same time, I know that my father did not want his children to have to fight the same fight and I did not want my children to have to fight this fight. But they do. And I know that Mandy (Kanahus), who along with her twin sister Nikki (Mayuk), her younger sister Anita Rose (Snutetkwe) and her brother Ska7cis, are all profoundly engaged in our struggle while at the same time hoping that their children do not have to face what they continue to face.

PART 3
EUROPEAN LAND CLAIMS

CHAPTER 8

WE STOLE IT FAIR AND SQUARE

There was and still is method to your madness. It was and still is about the land. The forces of cultural genocide that you launched against us were not because you are all wantonly cruel people (although some of you obviously were), it was because only by destroying us could you have uncontested ownership of the land. But we are still here demanding justice, demanding to know how we went from enjoying 100 per cent of our land to impoverishment and despair on 0.2 per cent of our land. How did a small country like Great Britain end up not only controlling but transmitting to its successor states "radical title" to the entire landmass of North America north of the Rio Grande?

For Indigenous peoples that answer is pretty clear: they stole it. That was their intention and that is what they did. They were simply following Pope Nicholas V's charter authorization of what amounted to European gangsterism. That, in a nutshell, is your history and our history together.

But this causes difficulties for your courts and the rule of law in general. For a long time Canadian governments and courts avoided addressing the question altogether and the joke among our people had rednecks responding simply: Okay, we stole it. But we stole it fair and square.

But as the court cases go forward, recognizing the principle of Aboriginal title and rights in the Delgamuukw decision in 1997, and Aboriginal title and rights on the ground, as in the Tsilhqot'in decision in 2014 — both of which we will look at in more detail later — the courts have been forced to address that issue, or at least find something more sophisticated than "we stole it fair and square" to justify European title. It has not been an easy task.

Historically, the legal underpinning for Crown title has been the doctrine of *terra nullius* and the doctrine of discovery, but for modern courts both are extremely problematic. After all, *terra nullius* suggests that the European land claim rests on the fact that the land was empty when they arrived — which is patently not the case. Most Europeans were met by Indigenous peoples almost instantly, often within minutes of setting foot on the shores of North America. The land was far from empty, inhabited by most estimates by tens of millions of peoples, with most modern estimates putting the combined population of North and South America around fifty-five million people — roughly the same as the population of Europe at the time.

Since the Americas were no more *terra nullius* than Europe, the justification was that *nullius* referred to the fact that the people were non-Christian. Which takes us back to Pope Nicholas V's papal bull in the mid-1450s authorizing Christian kings to enslave people and seize their lands and goods in any non-Christian territory.

Courts today are understandably reluctant to base their own legitimacy and the legitimacy of the state they are part of on a law that authorized gangsterism, piracy, theft, slavery, rape and murder, but there is not a lot left for them in trying to justify Crown title to these lands. That is why the Supreme Court tries to pull a rabbit out of their hat in justifying Crown title by citing an almost magical "European assertion of sovereignty." In the case of British Columbia, which I am most familiar with, this assertion was said to have been made in 1846 with the Treaty of Oregon, which set the southern boundary of British Columbia at a time when it was known as the Columbia District of the Hudson's Bay Company.

This is a convenient beginning for the "assertion of sovereignty" but it really begs the question. By what right were the British, and the Americans for that matter, able to negotiate a boundary line on lands that were not theirs and to put themselves in a position to assert their sovereignty? Of course it makes no legal sense. It is still theft by any other name. In his definitive study, "Sovereignty's Alchemy: An Analysis of Delgamuukw v. British Columbia," John Borrows examines these "non-consensual colonial assertions of Crown sovereignty."

He points out that "It does not make sense that one could secure a legal entitlement to land over another merely through raw assertion. As Chief Justice Marshall of the United States Supreme Court once observed, it is an 'extravagant and absurd idea.' It is even less of a 'morally and politically defensible' position when this assertion has not been a neutral and noble statement, but has benefited the Crown to the detriment of the land's original inhabitants."

In identifying the origins of Aboriginal title, the Crown says that it "crystallized" at the time European sovereignty was asserted. In other words, there was no title at all until the Crown asserted its own title, and at that time the concept of Aboriginal title appeared, as if out of thin air.

As Borrows observed:

> The Court might as well speak of magic
> crystals being sprinkled on the land as a
> justification for the diminution of Aboriginal
> occupation and possession. Crown title
> simply does not make sense to Aboriginal
> people (and one suspects to many non-
> Aboriginal people). The contemporary reli-
> ance on assertions of sovereignty seems to
> perpetuate the historical injustice suffered by
> aboriginal peoples at the hands of colonizers
> who failed to respect the distinctive cultures
> of pre-existing aboriginal societies.
>   Given that Aboriginal peoples in Brit-
> ish Columbia were not conquered and never
> agreed to diminish their governmental rights,
> Aboriginal sovereignty should be placed on
> at least the same, if not greater, footing as
> Crown sovereignty. It would be interesting
> to subject the Court's treatment of Crown
> sovereignty to the same standards it expects
> for evidence of Aboriginal self-government.

Borrows continued:

> Despite overwhelming numerical strength,
> they did not participate in the province's
> creation. Most Aboriginal peoples contin-
> ued to live within their own governments
> on their lands, as they had done for centu-
> ries, with little regard for British assertions

of sovereignty. In these circumstances, the words of United States Supreme Court Justice John Marshall are worth recalling:

"It is difficult to comprehend the proposition, that the inhabitants of either quarter of the globe could have rightful original claims of dominion over the inhabitants of the other, or over the lands they occupied; or that the discovery of either by the other should give the discoverer rights in the country discovered, which annulled the pre-existing rights of its ancient possessors."

That, finally, is the legal bedrock. No schemes of *terra nullius* or doctrine of discovery or assertion of sovereignty can legitimize morally or legally such a blatant land grab. All of the assertions and doctrines when boiled down can be reduced to "We stole it fair and square."

But this is not a solid base on which you can build legal title. This is legal quicksand. And that is the foundation upon which Canada is founded.

If you cannot explain this acquisition other than by theft, how can the legal system be founded on a criminal act? You will perhaps point to the treaties, many of which are themselves very questionable on what, exactly, they ceded, but how then do you explain the Crown acquiring the lands of the peoples of the Interior of British Columbia and many other parts of the country where treaties have not been signed? What is the legal mechanism for your having the right to inhabit it?

You know there is none. Because it was based on the lie of discovery with the confused European wanderers claiming all of the land from a river mouth to its source at an undetermined place in the interior — in the case of the Fraser River this meant hundreds of miles inland. This made for a ludicrous situation in which our lands and our nations were legally subject to the white man sometimes for a century before a white man even made it into our territory. How can that possibly be? And where, exactly, in this charade did they acquire legal title?

The court understands how that alchemy happened, how bumping into became discovery and discovery became overlordship. It was made possible through the quicksilver of racism, that black magic of white supremacy. The same substance that was behind the completely "legal" slave trade, the cultural genocide that followed is an attempt to forever destroy our people and our right to our lands. This theft of a continent is the crime of a millennium.

The courts themselves seem to recognize this because they have been prodding the government to negotiate a new deal with Indigenous peoples that will finally give the Crown legitimacy. But the political branch remains as deaf to those pleas as it does to ours.

CHAPTER 9

ATTEMPTED GENOCIDE: POLITICAL BATTLES WITH PIERRE TRUDEAU

When I confront the shape-shifting positions of Justin Trudeau, there is a personal note. This is the second generation of my family's battles with the Trudeaus. My father spent more than a decade battling Pierre Trudeau and his plans to strip of us of our rights in the name of liberty. I am increasingly fearful that Justin Trudeau has the same goal, but this time in the name of reconciliation.

That is my fear. But part of the reason that I have hope today is that my parents' generation, after a long and bitter battle, fended off Trudeau the Elder and finally even managed to open a crack in the constitutional strongbox with an explicit recognition of Aboriginal rights and title.

The first battle, which has been much written about, was Trudeau's plan to erase Indigenous peoples as a founding people in the infamous 1969 White Paper.

I wrote extensively about that fight in *Unsettling Canada*, but at the heart of it was the White Paper plan to sweep aside Indian status and Indian lands and turn Indians into ethnic groups to be absorbed into the melting pot. Any services to Indigenous peoples would be turned over to the provinces, and

existing treaties would be wound down. In one of its most cynical aspects, it echoed civil rights language to deny the national
rights of the sixty Indigenous nations within Canada. In the
cheerful words of the White Paper, the policy would "enable
the Indian people to be free — free to develop Indian cultures
in an environment of legal, social and economic equality with
other Canadians." What they were "freeing" us from was any
and all of our Aboriginal title and rights to the point where we
became "equal" to other ethnic groups in Canada.

That battle precipitated my father, George Manuel,
into the presidency of the newly-formed National Indian
Brotherhood with a prolonged protest against Trudeau
the Elder and his lead Indian fighter Jean Chrétien, which
culminated in Indigenous people ceremonially returning
the White Paper to Chrétien and replacing it with Harold
Cardinal's Red Paper.

The second major battle between my father and his
generation against Prime Minister Pierre Trudeau came in
1980 when Trudeau committed to patriating the *BNA Act*,
the Canadian Constitution, that was still only a document
passed by the British at Westminster. At that time my father
had moved on from the national chief's role and he was trying
to build a peoples movement within the Union of B.C. Indian
Chiefs. When he heard of the new Trudeau constitutional
gambit he was instantly worried that Trudeau was planning
to shut the door to us for all time in the *Charter of Rights*, that
would insist that no Canadian could be treated any differently
than any other Canadian. The 1969 White Paper, after all,
had been a policy to assimilate us into the Canadian community without any political or constitutional rights as distinct
peoples. So he launched a massive lobbying effort in Ottawa
and Europe to force Canada to include recognition of a third

order of government — Indigenous government, along with federal and provincial — in the Constitution.

As the president of the Union of B.C. Indian Chiefs, my father organized a train from Vancouver to Ottawa, which became known as the Constitution Express, to take the protest to Parliament Hill. Along the way, they raised such consciousness amongst Indigenous peoples that the train was literally stopped in northern parts of Ontario so people could give them moose stew and bannock as Indigenous people started to become aware that the constitutional framework was something that was vitally important to them. This mass lobbying effort was then extended to Europe in the European Constitution Express.

It was because of these intense political activities that Section 35, recognizing Aboriginal rights, was inserted into the repatriated Constitution. It states that "the existing

Canadian Constitution Act 1982
3 Orders of Goverment

35. (1) The existing aboriginal and treaty rights of the aboriginal peoples of Canada are hereby recongnized and affirmed.

Indigenous peoples finally enter Canada's founding document in Section 35.(1).

aboriginal and treaty rights of the aboriginal peoples of Canada are hereby recognized and affirmed."

But what has too often been forgotten is another section, Section 37, which was a companion to Section 35. And this is crucial to where we are today. This was where our precise place in the Canadian constitutional framework, as a founding people with an inherent right to govern ourselves, was supposed to be hammered out.

In Section 37, Canada was committed to holding a constitutional conference or series of conferences with Indigenous peoples themselves to define the content of our Section 35 rights. As it was written in the new Canadian Constitution:

> 37. (1) A constitutional conference composed of the Prime Minister of Canada and the first ministers of the provinces shall be convened by the Prime Minister of Canada within one year after this Part comes into force.
>
> (2) The conference convened under subsection (1) shall have included in its agenda an item respecting constitutional matters that directly affect the aboriginal peoples of Canada, including the identification and definition of the rights of those peoples to be included in the Constitution of Canada, and the Prime Minister of Canada shall invite representatives of those peoples to participate in the discussions on that item.

In this, the Constitution was setting out a framework to begin the decolonization of Canada, just as the Constitution itself had been a final symbolic act of the decolonization of Canada from Britain.

There were, in fact, not one but four such conferences held between 1983 and 1987 with the mandate of defining our self-governing rights and enshrining them in the Canadian Constitution. But each of these conferences ended in failure. Despite the promise in the Constitution to "recognize and affirm" Aboriginal rights, it soon became apparent that the federal and many of the provincial governments were attempting to "ignore and deny" our rights.

In both of the conferences held under the Trudeau government and those held under Brian Mulroney's Progressive Conservative government, the Canadian state proposed, instead of recognition of our inherent Aboriginal right to self-government, the same sort of a municipal-style government that is on the table at today's negotiating tables.

Indigenous representatives at the conference, which included representatives of the First Nations, the Inuit and Métis people, steadfastly rejected this diminution of our rights and insisted that recognition of Aboriginal and treaty rights in the Constitution had to include recognition of our inherent right to self-government.

Between these two positions — recognition of constitutionally protected self-governing peoples and the colonialist package from the federal and provincial governments — the differences were irreconcilable. And they still are. Reconciliation then and now is only possible if we abandon our rights, which have since been enshrined in the UN Declaration of the Rights of Indigenous Peoples, or if the government recognizes our land rights and our fundamental right to self-determination. Without that, all of the hugs and tears, and increases in program and service money are meaningless. But in 1987, we were not even offered hugs.

At the end of the negotiations, the federal minister of justice and attorney general, Ray Hnatyshyn, flatly rejected the idea that our peoples had a right to "self-determination." He said that this was the same as demanding sovereign rights, and sovereignty applied only to Canada as a whole. Period.

On the Indigenous side, there was a kind of shock that the decolonization process that Section 35 was supposed to address had been blocked by the Canadian political class. But for the federal and provincial governments, the failure of the negotiations was the intended outcome, the prerequisite for their colonial business-as-usual approach with sweeping the rights of Indigenous peoples under Canada's constitutional carpet with the vague assertion that these issues could be sifted through by the courts in some undetermined future.

But this was offering Indigenous people a constitutional merry-go-round. The politicians said they would leave the courts to spell out the rights they themselves refused to spell out in the document that the court would use to determine our rights. In fact, the fundamental change needed to decolonize Canada is beyond the domestic capacity of the Supreme Court of Canada to decide. But as we have seen in case after case, the Supreme Court has decided substantially in favour of Indigenous rights on virtually every issue and it has at times even pleaded with the government to begin to act fairly and lawfully toward Indigenous peoples. That is where we remain today. The remedy should be to force the government to sit down with Indigenous representatives and restart the Section 37 negotiations it walked away from in 1987. Their tactic has instead been to refuse to talk about our rights — only thinking how they will extinguish them. So as we shall see later, we have been forced to go to the international level to seek justice.

CHAPTER 10

CHANGING LEGAL AND POLICY LANDSCAPE — 1984–2014

A crucial part of our struggle takes place in the courts. I know that the legal issues can be difficult to slog through but I am afraid it is essential if you are to understand where we are as Indigenous peoples in Canada. So please be prepared to put on your hip waders for the next several pages to accompany me across this legal swamp. I promise there is higher and drier land later on in this book, but crossing this swamp is the only way to gain the understanding we will need to get to our destination. And if you manage to stay alert, you might even catch sight of the rare beauty of the law when it also touches on justice. But as my law school professors sadly admitted, Canada does not have a justice system, it has a legal system.

In Aboriginal law, the courts have been trying to signal to Canada that there are grave legal problems in its Indian policies that must be addressed. The government has ignored them, but the courts have not only continued their calls for fundamental change on the side of the executive branch, they have escalated them.

The first signal from the court that all was not well with

Canada's Indian policy came way back in 1973 with the so-called Calder decision, where the Supreme Court split on the idea that Aboriginal title had survived Confederation to remain a burden on Crown title. At the time, the decision sent shockwaves through the Canadian polity because it was widely assumed that Indigenous people had no rights whatsoever and we had been reduced to the status of, in the insulting words of pre-War commentators, a "subject race."

Pierre Trudeau famously responded to the Calder decision by proclaiming, "Perhaps you have more legal rights than we thought . . ." His response was to send his Indian fighter, Jean Chrétien, to the justice department to devise legal instruments to quickly and cheaply terminate whatever title existed. This was the origin of the comprehensive claims process, and the first claim to be decided was that of the James Bay Cree who were pressured into either signing a cede, release and surrender deal for their lands or having them seized by Hydro Quebec without compensation.

The James Bay agreement became the model for the "modern treaties," which include the treaties in the north, the Nisga'a settlement in B.C. and the ongoing British Columbian treaty negotiations known as the B.C. Commission Treaty process. All of them, in one formulation or another, demand that we extinguish our rights to our homelands.

This process has not only been criticized by United Nations human rights bodies, it has been put under serious question by Canada's Supreme Court. The court has continued to evolve on the question of Aboriginal title and rights, especially after the 1982 patriation of the Constitution with a new Section 35 recognizing and affirming existing Aboriginal title and rights.

The first clear legal breakthrough on our Section 35 rights came with the Supreme Court's Delgamuukw decision. That case was begun in 1984 by the Gitksan and the Wet'suwet'en nations, who claimed ownership and legal jurisdiction over 133 individual hereditary territories, a total of 58,000 square kilometres of northwestern British Columbia — an area larger than the province of Nova Scotia. The Supreme Court decision on December 11, 1997, recognized Aboriginal title "as a right to the land itself" and was for Indigenous peoples a two-steps-forward moment. The court did not rule on the title on the ground, but it did recognize the principle of Aboriginal title as a form of ownership that included economic rights. The court also recognized our oral tradition as legitimate evidence in court.

The decision, written primarily by Chief Justice Antonio Lamer, provided Indigenous peoples from unceded Aboriginal title territories with their first clear legal foundation and, consequently, an historic opportunity to attain the justice that our ancestors had been struggling for centuries to achieve.

A few years later, in 2004, the Supreme Court of Canada's Haida Nation decision moved the legal cause forward still further by establishing legal principles around the Crown's duty to consult and accommodate Aboriginal rights and title on an interim basis until the matter is resolved in a more permanent manner through agreement, treaty or litigation.

The advances in the courts have continued to run up against a brick wall in the political sphere. Even into the present, the federal government has refused to change its comprehensive claims policy regarding land rights to make it consistent with the Delgamuukw decision or the Haida decision. They still demand extinguishment of our title as the first principle of any land deal.

We can see from the table below that the shape of these agreements are not really negotiated (in the usual sense of two parties sitting down and going through a give and take) at all. They are, instead, cookie-cutter agreements aimed at getting rid of the Indian problem for as little money and land concessions as possible with all real power deposited back in the firm control of the federal and provincial governments — kind of a revenge of Section 91/92. The only significant change in the agreements that followed the 1999 Nisga'a agreement is

Cookie Cutter Agreements	Nisga's Final Agrement (Sq Km)	Tsaw-wassen AiP (Hectare)	Yale AiP (Hectare)	Lheidi T'enneh AiP (Hect-are)	Yekooche AiP (Hectare)	Sliam-mon AiP (Hectare)	Maa-nulth AiP (Hectare)
Application of the Constitution Of Canada	Yes	Yes	Yes	Yes	Yes	Yes	Yes
Application of Federal & Provincial Laws	Yes	Yes	Yes	Yes	Yes	Yes	Yes
Restriction of Section 35 Rights	Yes	Yes	Yes	Yes	Yes	Yes	Yes
Extinguishment through Modified Rights Model	Yes	Yes	Yes	Yes	Yes	Yes	Yes
Release of Past Claims	Yes	Yes	Yes	Yes	Yes	Yes	Yes
Application of Provincial Laws	Yes	Yes	Yes	Yes	Yes	Yes	Yes
Extinguishment through the Land Selection Process	1,932	365	915.2	3,154	5,960	5,121	20,900
Termination Indian Reserves	Yes	Yes	Yes	Yes	Yes	Yes	Yes
Aboriginal Title Converted to Free Simple	Yes	Yes	Yes	Yes	Yes	Yes	Yes
Elimination of Section 87 Tax Exemption	Yes	Yes	Yes	Yes	Yes	Yes	Yes

16-04-29   2006

Cookie cutter agreements: negotiations are a charade when the exact result is determined beforehand.

that the terms have been getting worse for Indigenous peoples, with less and less land being allocated.

Canada's unwillingness then and now to change comprehensive land claims and self-government policies, both of which demand that we surrender our Aboriginal title and rights, indicate that Canada accepts no fundamental change to be made to our impoverishment. Administering to Indigenous peoples through the dependency programs is an expenditure to maintain Canada and the provinces' 99.8 per cent control of our Aboriginal and treaty territories. But by this time, the United Nations was watching. After 1975, the United Nations said to Canada, "You cannot ask indigenous people to extinguish their title as part of a land settlement agreement." No people in the world has the right to demand another people surrender their land to them.

So Canada had to figure out how to meet the UN requirement and still get control of our land. The Indian Affairs minister brought all the bright deputy ministers and high priced consultants together and asked them: "How can we extinguish Aboriginal title without using the word extinguishment?"

The bureaucrats have provided a seemingly endless stream of euphemisms and Orwellian distortions for what they are actually doing. One of the more recent was the "modified rights" model. According to this model, Indigenous people would be forced to "modify" their rights so they no longer included what we understood as Aboriginal title. They don't extinguish our title out of existence, instead they modify it out of existence.

They are still pulling the same stunts. Now that "modified rights" have become as discredited as extinguishment, they are beginning to speak about "reconciling Aboriginal rights"

with the broader Canadian economic purposes, which basically means that a treaty agreement with the government
will supersede Section 35.1 and, once again, free us from the
heavy burden of our Aboriginal title and rights.

It can all get very confusing, especially when you're
trying to explain this to grassroots people, who use
language with integrity. In the government's hands yes
means no and no means yes. Title is acknowledged in one
breath and then disappears from the table in the next.
At one point they even called the negotiating process,
"surrender and grant back." Suggesting that to begin the
negotiations Indigenous peoples had to surrender all of
their rights and then the government would decide which
of our rights it would "grant back." When negotiating
with the government you try to follow the pea under the
walnut and only after you sign do you realize that the
walnut, the pea and your title have all simply disappeared
into the government pocket.

But in recent years, the federal government's priority
has been to accelerate the settlement of final agreements
with the actively negotiating nations — and it intends to
use all final agreements reached with the actively negotiating nations as precedents against Indigenous nations
not negotiating.

On September 4, 2012, the federal government let fall
any pretence of seeking compromise or reform when it
announced the "results-based" approach to modern treaty
(comprehensive claims) and self-government agreements.
Henceforth, the federal government would only deal with
bands that, in effect, agree to surrender before the negotiations continue. To be included in the future negotiations,
bands would be required to:

Accept the extinguishment (modification) of
Aboriginal Title;
Accept the legal release of Crown liability for
past violations of Aboriginal Title & Rights;
Accept elimination of Indian Reserves by
accepting lands in fee simple;
Accept removing on-reserve tax exemptions;
Respect existing Third Party Interests (and
therefore alienation of Aboriginal Title terri-
tory without compensation);
Accept (to be assimilated into) existing federal
& provincial orders of government;
Accept application of Canadian Charter of
Rights & Freedoms over governance & insti-
tutions in all matters;
Accept Funding on a formula basis being
linked to own source revenue;
Other measures, and accept becoming
Aboriginal municipalities.

In a staggering case of déjà vu, the 2012 policy
followed the broad lines of the White Paper policy
of 1969. And the new Trudeau government simply
adopted the 2012 Harper policy, which in fact was based
on Liberal government strategies going back to 1973
when the Supreme Court initially kicked the can of
Indigenous rights in the direction of the government.
The line between Pierre Trudeau to Brian Mulroney
to Jean Chrétien to Stephen Harper to the next generation Trudeau is sadly unbroken and unchanged. Stealing
Indigenous land is a decidedly non-partisan, intergenerational activity in Canada.

So what does all this mean to our people who sign these agreements? I do not need magic to tell you where, exactly, they will be in forty years.

I know, because in October 2015 I was watching television with the sound off and I saw an Indigenous woman speaking.

I turned up the sound. She was one of the Cree women who was interviewed in a Radio Canada report on the situation in Val d'Or. The woman said that over the past twenty years, poor and homeless Indigenous women were picked up by Sûreté du Québec (SQ) officers for being drunk and driven to the woods outside of town. Some say they were paid or given alcohol or drugs to perform sex acts with police officers. Others said they were beaten or sexually assaulted and then abandoned by the police.

The Cree woman said, "Instead of taking me to the police station, they took me someplace else. They'd ask me, 'Do you want some beer?' They had some in their trunk. They'd give me one, then another, then another. And we'd drive into the little roads here, and stop by the side. That's where they'd ask me to give them a blowjob . . ." She said this happened to virtually every Native girl who was on the streets.

In the following days, more and more Indigenous women came forward to complain about similar and even far worse abuse by the police — including repeated sexual assaults — and of the general contempt they often faced from people in the city where they had been driven because of the poverty of their reserves of Waswanipi, and coastal Cree communities such as Waskaganish, Chisasibi, Wemindji, Nemaska and Eastmain.

This all came to light exactly forty years after the James Bay Cree signed their comprehensive claim agreement with

Canada and the Quebec government. And that agreement is almost identical to the "modern treaties" that Indigenous peoples signed in the north and that are being sold to Indigenous people in British Columbia today — if anything they are even less generous than the James Bay agreement.

So there you are. This is what our future will be like forty years after signing a land claim agreement with Canada. The result will be the same poverty, and the most outrageous forms of abuse that the Cree of Northern Québec have suffered for the past forty years and under the current system will stretch into perpetuity.

As a final insult in the Val d'Or case, not one single police officer was charged for their outrageous criminal acts against the Cree women. This is what Pierre Trudeau gave to us in the land claims agreements, what every Liberal and Conservative leader since has offered us and what Justin Trudeau is trying to foist on us. He can cry a tear, almost at will, for our pitiful state, but he is as ruthless as the others in keeping us there with his inherited extinguishment policies that seize our land and leave us in poverty and despair.

CHAPTER 11
TSILHQOT'IN CASE AND CROWN TITLE

The Canadian government holds on to its refusal to recognize Aboriginal title even in the face of the landmark Tsilhqot'in Nation v. British Columbia Supreme Court decision.

The Tsilhqot'in decision was delivered on June 26, 2014, and it picked up where Delgamuukw left off with the first ever declaration of Aboriginal title on the ground in Canadian history. By granting this powerful remedy and recognizing the existence of Aboriginal title over a two thousand square hectare section of Tsilhqot'in territory, the court has shown that extinguishment is far from the only option in Canada. The court also found that the government's arguments were based on the erroneous theory that Aboriginal title could only be established on a site-specific basis — over a specific fishing or hunting area, for example. The Tsilhqot'in decision found it was much broader, encompassing, for example, thousands of hectares of territory. In effect, federal and provincial laws and policies that are still based on this erroneous theory actually fail to recognize Aboriginal title altogether.

The Tsilhqot'in decision was a major victory in an almost unbroken string of court victories for Indigenous peoples since 1973. But while the Supreme Court's Tsilhqot'in decision can be used in many ways to advance our struggle to have our Aboriginal title and rights recognized and respected, the decision is still a decision of a colonial court and, as such, again reflects the fact that the whole of the Crown's own claim to our territories is still grounded on legal quicksand.

This is an important point and I know it sounds confusing to some. Of course we hail court decisions that move the yardsticks forward in recognizing our rights and title — often by a considerable distance — and we urge the government to respect their own laws. But we still must point out that we need a political deal to finally decolonize, because the court cannot, finally, admit that the Crown has no legal basis to our lands because the court is itself part of the Crown (made up of the executive, legislative and judicial branches) and would therefore undercut its own legal basis to exist. So even in the Tsilhqot'in decision, which is light-years ahead of where the government is, the Supreme Court says:

> At the time of assertion of European sover-
> eignty, the Crown acquired radical or under-
> lying title to all the land in the province. This
> Crown title, however, was burdened by the
> pre-existing legal rights of Aboriginal people
> who occupied and used the land prior to
> European arrival.

Here the court is saying, without any explanation or reasoned argument, that settler property rights are higher than Indigenous property rights. In fact, there is no "reason" at all, as Borrows has pointed out. What is at its heart is racism — the idea that white people have the inherent right to claim title to Indigenous lands, or the lands of black or brown peoples, and rule them as colonial masters. The final unspoken argument is always racism. There is simply no other explanation for claiming Crown title is radical title and Aboriginal title is a "burden" on it.

But with this racist declaration on the ownership of our lands, the government still manages to manipulate our leadership into negotiating these dead-end, go nowhere kind of agreements, like the treaty and reconciliation framework agreements that we will look at later.

Canadians had gotten away with this kind of doublespeak 150 years ago, but we cannot let them continue to rely on the property concept that insists that white man's or settlers' property rights supersede Indigenous property rights. This is founded on the colonial concept that the queen somehow acquired "radical or underlying title" when Britain declared it so under British colonial constitutional and legal doctrines. The fact that these constitutional and legal colonial concepts survived for 150-some years does not make them legitimate any more than slave laws in Europe and the Americas that persisted for four hundred years.

Our leadership must continually assert that Aboriginal title is the underlying title in our territory and that all other property rights are layers of property rights that rest on underlying Aboriginal title. Our own leadership needs to change the fundamental concept of underlying title before we can change the way property laws are made in our territory.

At present, all property law legislation operating in our territory, like the *Mining Act, Parks Act, Municipal Act, Land Title Act* and all other such acts are based on the provincial claim to having underlying title. We can legally challenge this in the future, but first we need to show that the idea of Canada acquiring underlying title is a colonial and racist idea and no more valid than the racist Jim Crow laws in the American south or the legal framework that grew up around the international slave trade. They are unjust laws and morally indefensible.

It is indicative of where we are today that an incomplete decision like the Tsilhqot'in decision is still far too progressive for our government to even consider. In fact, the shock of the recognition of our territorial rights on the ground led to the government hurriedly commissioning the so-called Eyford Report on reforming the land claims policy. We will look at the report in more detail, but it was basically another poorly conceived attempt to keep alive what even the courts have ruled is a failed policy.

I can see that some pro-settler Indigenous leaders like Jody Wilson-Raybould, who has joined the Trudeau team as Minister of Justice, will try to use Tsilhqot'in to prop up rather than to bury their ailing treaty process — largely by changing the vocabulary but not the policy. To counter this, we must use the decision to force dramatic changes in the government negotiating process, eliminating once and for all the comprehensive land claims policy and its unrelenting push toward extinguishment, which has been denounced by the United Nations for the past forty years. That is how much of an outlier the Trudeau government actually is. It refuses to acknowledge the international rulings regarding our rights, and even refuses to acknowledge its own Supreme Court rulings regarding our rights by Justin's father's forty-year-old extinguishment land claims policy. It is our job to force Canada to catch up and move ahead into true decolonization.

CHAPTER 12

BRITISH COLUMBIA COMMISSION TREATY PROCESS

As I said at the outset, I know for many of you this legal slogging is hard going. Wading through Canadian Aboriginal law is not easy. And if this were a public meeting, right about now I know I would see people glancing out the window or surreptitiously checking their phones. And if we were meeting in a church basement or legion hall, I would suggest a coffee break so we could stretch our legs and maybe have a quick cigarette out on the sidewalk. But I promise you we are more than halfway across the legal swamp, so we have to continue — if only for a few more minutes — to complete the journey. Because if we are going to stand up to the intellectual assault our opponents are relentlessly hitting us with, it is essential that we know not only that our cause is just, but exactly why it is just and all of the ways that governments and their handmaidens, at places like the Fraser Institute and on the editorial boards of the major newspapers, try to manipulate us with false logic and foggy language to tell us we do not have any rights at all other than those that, in their generosity, they deem to grant us.

So please stay with me for a few more short sections, then we can leave the swamp to climb back onto more solid ground.

But first we have to examine one of the ugliest beasts of all in the government's land claims sham. It is called the B.C. Commission Treaty process and what it is offering to us, and to the watching world, as the final resolution — I almost want to say final solution — to our land claims, and the final answer to what has long been known as "the B.C. land question."

The B.C. land claims negotiation process was started in the wake of the 1990 Oka stand-off by a government that feared the uprising might spread west. The B.C. process would be devoted to resolving "outstanding issues — including claims to un-extinguished Aboriginal rights — with British Columbia's First Nations." The new process did not come with new ideas, however. The model then, as now, was the comprehensive claims policy of Pierre Trudeau (with Brian Mulroney's 1986 revisions), which was designed as and remains the main instrument to extinguish our rights.

Since then, First Nations have been negotiating under this B.C. treaty process for more than two decades with very little success. Only two agreements have been finalized. The reason is simple: the federal government has kept the benefits so low and they demand so much — in effect the extinguishment of our Aboriginal title and rights — that negotiators know they could not get support for a deal from their own people. Therefore the negotiations go on and on and never bear fruit. In fact, the existing policy has been very expensive in terms of money as well as time. Negotiations have been taking place over the last twenty-one years and cost over a billion dollars, of which more than $500 million dollars has been borrowed by the impoverished Indigenous communities. On the road to our own extinguishment, we also dig financial graves with these negotiating debts. To continue along this path is not only pointless, it is madness.

In essence, the extinguishment of Aboriginal title and rights through the "cede, release and surrender" model, then the "surrender and grant back" model, then the "modification" model and the "non-assertion" model and finally the current "reconciliation" model are all forms of genocide because they break the link between Indigenous peoples and their ownership and jurisdiction over their lands. Canada must understand that only through the recognition of Aboriginal title and rights will we be able to move together toward a better and more prosperous Canada.

What we have seen instead is Canada flailing around to re-assert its failed and internationally condemned extinguishment model under different names. To accomplish this in the immediate aftermath of the Tsilhqot'in decision, the government commissioned the Eyford Report, after its author Douglas Eyford — officially known by the awkward-sounding "Renewing the Comprehensive Land Claims Policy: Towards a Framework for Addressing Section 35 Aboriginal Rights." The report was written for Indigenous peoples who are negotiating under the federal government's existing comprehensive land claims policy. My community of Neskonlith has never negotiated under the existing policy, so we are not involved in the negotiation problems the policy is supposed to be addressing, but we are nonetheless deeply impacted by the existing comprehensive land claims policy.

The two provisions in the Eyford Report that affect us are "self-government negotiations" and "negotiations of non-treaty agreements." Both these polices are unacceptable.

In the Eyford Report, self-government claims to be part of our "inherent right" to govern ourselves, but it is top-down delegated authority — like the relationship of municipalities to the provincial governments — that does not take into account our right to self-determination as Indigenous peoples. The negotiation of non-treaty agreements may sound like a big step forward from the restrictive treaty policies, but it clearly states that the mandate to negotiate under these non-treaty negotiations would be limited to the same mandate as the treaty and self-government processes.

This report does not provide any fundamental change to the existing comprehensive land claims policy. It will not change anything except to make economic uncertainty more intense in Secwepemc territory. You cannot have the courts recognize Aboriginal title on the ground in our neighbouring territory of the Tsilhqot'in Nation and then use a new version of the comprehensive land claims policy to remove Aboriginal title from Secwepemc lands. We are not fools. This go-nowhere kind of policy leads us to believe that once again Canada is shutting its door to serious negotiations, and we will only find justice at the international level.

We must remember that Section 35 and Section 37 were added to the Canadian *Constitution Act, 1982* because of the Constitution Express in 1980, and the Constitution Express lobby in Britain, Europe and the United Nations in NYC, which brought our protest not only to Ottawa but to world capitals. The Eyford Report is proof of how little distance Canada is prepared to go in addressing the question of our rights in the wake of the Supreme Court of Canada's declaration of Aboriginal title for the Tsilhqot'in Nation. Our only honourable response, for those who have been in negotiation with the government on the basis of any variation of the extinguishment-driven comprehensive claims policy, is to stand up and walk away.

My community, Neskonlith, will not even sit down with the federal government under the British Columbia treaty process. We will not negotiate with the federal government under the federal comprehensive land claims policy — not because we do not want to negotiate, or because we do not want to talk, or because we do not want to come to some mutual agreement on development in our territory. No, we won't sit down with the federal government when their policy is to extinguish our Aboriginal title and rights. We just will not sit down with anybody whose idea is to extinguish us, to commit genocide against us. We won't sit down with them until they take our extinguishment off the table.

This is the minimum of what we asked from Justin Trudeau. But he, apparently, has decided that he is here to do his father's work — to extinguish the rights of Indigenous peoples on Canadian lands in exchange for a few more programs and services, which he offers with crocodile tears over our 150 years of "misfortune."

CHAPTER 13
RIGHTFUL TITLE HOLDERS

Political power in our communities remains under federal jurisdiction and our political institutions are still lashed to the 1867 constitutional framework of Section 91.24. In B.C., this makes it very complicated because Indigenous peoples have never surrendered their Aboriginal title off the Indian reserves, which has been confirmed on several occasions by the Supreme Court of Canada.

One vitally important legal issue that is coming to the fore — with great implications for our struggle down the line — is who exactly is the rightful title holder?

This was an important issue in the Delgamuukw decision, where it was the hereditary chiefs who brought the case forward and not the elected Indian Act chiefs. The hereditary chiefs in many Indigenous nations in B.C. are actually family leaders for a family territory within the boundaries of their nation. In Delgamuukw, the Indian Act chiefs actually challenged the standing of the hereditary chiefs, but the courts ruled that it was the hereditary chiefs who had "locus standi."

This was also an issue in the Tsilhqot'in case, because that case was brought by the Nemiah Indian Band (Xeni Gwet'in) and the court was asked to rule on the question of who is the "rightful title holder." In this instance, the case was allowed to proceed but the issue of the rightful title holder was not clearly resolved. It was simply agreed that Aboriginal title is a collective right.

So who is the rightful title holder and who should represent their interests in court? Indian Act chiefs are problematic because they receive their power and authority from the Canadian government. So in representing the people they are, at best, representing two masters who are in direct conflict with one another. And one of those masters, the federal government, pays their salaries and funds virtually all of the programs they administer. Indian Act chiefs are further limited because their authority is specific to their reserve — that 0.2 per cent of Canada where the Indian Act devolves them their powers. Indian Act chiefs are very clearly defined in Canada's legal and constitutional framework as being a local delegated Indian authority with the powers to deal with such trivial matters as bees and dogs within the very limited territory of the reserve. How, then, can they suddenly represent nations off the reserve on their people's Indigenous territories, which is clearly outside of the purview of the *Indian Act* that created them?

The hereditary chief system avoids many of these pitfalls. Their traditional territories are distributed throughout the national territory, comprising all of the tribal lands. They receive their authority from tribal custom, and not the imposition of the *Indian Act* on their peoples by a foreign government. But the problem is that often the traditional hereditary system has been seriously or totally eradicated by the Indian Act system. In only a few cases does the hereditary chief system still have enough vigour to assert the people's sovereignty over their traditional territories.

Failing a robust hereditary chief system, it is up to the people themselves to make decisions collectively in large public meetings that are based not on the band, but on the nation. Because finally, it is the grassroots people who are collectively the indisputable title holders of our national territories.

This is one of the challenges for us today — to establish our own governments with a clear method for the title holders, the people themselves, to assert their rights and pursue our own economic, social and cultural goals free from the Indian Act system and federal jurisdiction under Section 91.24.

This is also why we need to be very careful about supporting any kind of federal or provincial legislation, policies or participation in programs and services where financial agreements concede jurisdiction to the granting federal and provincial government. All of these arrangements require us to surrender our own inherent governing powers and undermine our rights as title holders of our national territories. And this we should never do. What we must do is to confirm our court and other victories on the ground, which I will discuss in more detail in Part 7.

CHAPTER 14
RISK AND UNCERTAINTY

In these last two chapters of this section, we look at some of the important economic implications of the legal uncertainty over Crown ownership of the land.

Because in the final analysis, it is the legal uncertainty created by our assertion of our territorial rights and the Supreme Court decisions that recognize them that the federal government is attempting to remove in its extinguishment drive. And they are doing this because that legal uncertainty leads to massive economic uncertainty — some estimates put the amount of investment in resource extraction in Canada that is being held back by economic uncertainty over land claims at more than $600 billion (yes, billion). This is where we can find significant leverage for ourselves in our dealings with government.

The real crux of the problem is that Indigenous peoples and settlers have diametrically opposed interests in the land. Indigenous peoples own and control the land because of original occupation and use. The settlers want the land because they want to inhabit and economically control it and this struggle is constantly being fought in the constitutional, legal and political arenas and, increasingly, on the ground.

The battle has been an ever-shifting one. When Indigenous peoples were having considerable success in the 1920s in international lobbying for their rights in both London and Geneva, the Canadian government moved, in 1927, to make Indian land challenges illegal. So our political activism went underground, and the restrictions were lifted in the 1950s only when it was thought we had been beaten into submission with the crushing oppression, family break-ups and forced deculturation of the residential schools.

But since then our people have been undergoing a steady resurgence, and we are not only back to fighting in the constitutional, legal and political arenas and, especially, on the ground, we are winning many of the crucial battles.

This puts the whole question of federal and provincial legal control of Canadian territory in question. They still claim that they control 100 per cent of it, but they can no longer claim 100 per cent certainty of that fact, especially in places like British Columbia where they have no treaties.

It is very important to understand the term "certainty" and how it relates to the fact that Aboriginal title was found to exist by the Supreme Court of Canada in 1997, and that Aboriginal title is protected under the *Constitution Act, 1982*. Certainty must be looked at in context of economics.

The basis of uncertainty is the fact that Aboriginal title is protected by the *Constitution Act, 1982*. These legal and constitutional facts create uncertainty, because they potentially affect resource industries' access to our lands, where the resources are found. Provincially created property rights like mining permits and forestry licences did not and cannot extinguish Aboriginal title, because the province never had power over Indigenous peoples and territories.

This means that the province has never had the capacity
to give full title to anyone who holds provincial property. This is what is creating economic uncertainty. The
Canadian and British Columbian governments have been
trying to manage this uncertainty through the federal
comprehensive land claims policy and the B.C. treaty
process, but so far it has been a dismal failure. Agreements
of surrender are not being signed.

So because that uncertainty exists, it is a financial risk for
resource companies to come onto our land. They can never
know if they are one court judgement away from having
their multi-million and even billion dollar investments
seized by the legitimate title holders.

For us, this uncertainty and the risk it entails, both for
resource extractors operating on our territories and for the
government itself in its dealing with international creditors, provides important leverage in any negotiations with
the government. We know that behind the scenes both the
resource companies and the international investors are pushing the government to come to a deal with us. And they have
been for decades. As far back as 1990, Price Waterhouse
issued a report, "Economic Value of Uncertainty Associated
with Native Claims in B.C.," that found that land claims
created uncertainty in the mining industry and impacted
the B.C. economy in a major way. That awareness, and the
sense of urgency that a solution must be found, has grown
exponentially since then.

This is why we need to be so careful that our rights do
not get highjacked through quick cash deals, and instead we
need to address the broader issues collectively across B.C.
and Canada to have our title recognized by the government
before we even discuss access. It is irresponsible for us to

take a few dollars today to give access to a mine, and in doing so threaten the health of our land and our Aboriginal title, leaving our grandchildren politically weakened with an arsenic-laced tailings pond on their territory.

This is why we really need to talk at the community level about how we can address our poverty through Aboriginal title. Certainty means a lot more than just a media headline for big business and big government. It means that the poor in our community can be factored into the economy; not just as employees, but also, and more importantly, as title holders with responsibilities to protect the land while at the same time receiving benefits from our Aboriginal title territories.

The running 150-year-old battle for the land continues and, as the uncertainty of government control increases, so increases the risk to investors. The real problem is that the federal and provincial governments want to maintain the mutual exclusive control over Aboriginal and treaty territories and not recognize Aboriginal and treaty rights in a type of stable, mutually agreed-upon, shared jurisdiction that could, in fact, end the uncertainty. In essence, Canada is still pursuing the goal of extinguishing our Aboriginal rights and ignoring their treaty obligations and assimilating us into the settler-state society.

To address this, we need to develop our own risk analysis and management strategy that will counter the settler risk analysis and management strategy imposed by Canada and British Columbia. In our strategy, we must do everything possible to increase economic risk and undermine settler certainty.

We have to fight against our own extinguishment at every turn and with all of our energies. The last time we fought on these issues was during the Constitution Express of the 1980s. Before that was the fight against the 1969 White Paper. Both of these were national struggles against the extinguishment of our Aboriginal and treaty rights, and we need a similar kind of unity and commitment around these principles today. We need to begin by putting pressure on Canada and the provinces economically. We need to take advantage of the economic uncertainty that Aboriginal and treaty rights create, and take action to have these views considered by economic interests like credit-rating agencies, insurance companies and private landholders. I think that the 2008 global financial meltdown showed individuals that hidden economic decisions can affect the cost of houses. In this case, the hidden economic factors are Aboriginal and treaty rights and we have to let the world know that all is not what it seems in Canada's books. To prove it, we only have to point to the annual reports by British Columbia's auditor general.

CHAPTER 15

REVENGE OF THE BALANCE SHEET

Canadian governments are used to lying to Indigenous peoples and the Canadian public about what they are doing in Indigenous policies, but it is a little more difficult to lie to the creditors. The B.C. government is bound by international accounting practices to report how they're dealing with the Indigenous land issue on their balance sheets.

This is another aspect of risk that is just as problematic for the government as the uncertainty for the resource extractors. The B.C. finance minister has to report each year to the auditor general about how they are dealing with their liability to Indigenous peoples for our Aboriginal title. To mitigate the enormous potential financial problems this creates, the government assures the public and the lenders that the majority of Indigenous peoples are going to accept land from the province as settlements and that we are actually borrowing money from them to negotiate the extinguishment of our Aboriginal title. But the auditors general aren't so easily put off. They know that B.C. Indigenous nations can go to court to have their title recognized and this makes them, at the very least, a "contingent liability." And all contingent liabilities need to be reported on the province's books.

We get a clear idea of the auditor general's point of view from the November 2006 Report of the Auditor General of Canada to the House of Commons, which looked at the federal government's participation in the British Columbia treaty process. The report described "differing views" between the Indigenous peoples and the settlers. These "differing views" are rather quickly dealt with in the report, but go to the very crux of the problem that is causing all negotiations between Indigenous peoples and the settler governments to fail: the auditor general of Canada clearly identifies that "participants must share a common vision of their relationship and of the future" for negotiations to be successful. They say that this does not exist under the existing British Columbia treaty process.

The auditor general goes further to identify government intransigence as the main obstacle to the negotiations, by pointing out that the federal and provincial governments base their negotiations on "their own policies, and do not recognize the Aboriginal rights and title claimed by the First Nations." This means if we really believe in the federal and provincial governments recognizing and affirming our Aboriginal and treaty rights, we need to change the fundamental policy of the federal and provincial governments before we go to the table. We cannot negotiate if Canada and the provinces' ultimate plan is to not recognize existing rights and to extinguish Aboriginal and treaty rights.

So for many years, the government has been forced to list these claims on their financial statements as contingent liabilities. With the Supreme Court's 2014 Tsilhqot'in decision, this isn't a purely contingent liability any longer. It is a real liability, because Aboriginal title has been found to exist on the ground. The only issue is the amount — and with the Tsilhqot'in decision, the amount of that liability has skyrocketed.

The exact size of this liability could even have a significant impact on B.C. and Canada's credit rating.

We have been active in pursuing the implications internationally. As mentioned, my organization, the Indigenous Network on Economies and Trade (INET), submitted briefs to NAFTA and the World Trade Organization that asserted our proprietary interest in the timber resources on our Aboriginal title lands, and they were accepted by both bodies. Later, we met with Standard & Poor's in New York, and they said that clearly Canada was hiding things on its books under the contingent liabilities for Aboriginal title lands. Now with the Tsilhqot'in decision, that contingent liability has been magnified a hundred times and it is very close to being transformed into actual, quantifiable liability.

Until Canada settles with Indigenous peoples this accounting debt and overall economic uncertainty will hang over them like a sword of Damocles. And this sword is scaring away investors from Canada. As we assert our rights, more and more investors will pull out because of the uncertainty about resource development. If we continue to insist on asserting our rights, the only solution for the government will be at long last to begin good faith negotiations with us that do not begin with us surrendering our title, but have a goal of sharing this land in a way that ensures that we and Mother Earth, which we all depend on, are protected in perpetuity. We must have back not only what we need to survive, but to prosper under a system built not on domination but on mutual self-determination and respect. And ironically, the surest way to get to this point is to use the almighty balance sheet to force the government to deal with us. If we can make the cost of ignoring us higher than it is to deal with us, they will deal. That, finally, is the Canadian way. In a country founded on the balance sheet, the balance sheet is the only force that will lead to fundamental changes.

But before we can seriously embark on our full political and economic offensive, we ourselves have some house cleaning to do.

PART 4
PUTTING OUR OWN HOUSE IN ORDER

CHAPTER 16

NEOCOLONIALISM, OR SELLING OUR BIRTHRIGHT

The previous section looked at some complex issues. This one looks at some delicate ones — especially for Indigenous peoples, who hold respect toward all people as a deep and fundamental value. But sometimes frank talk is necessary. I have to say at the outset that I honestly mean no disrespect, but we cannot forever ignore the fact that some of our leaders, or people who speak in our name, are leading us toward oblivion.

While we have watched the rise of Indigenous movements devoted to taking back our land and sovereignty, there remain a small number of powerful Indigenous individuals who still seem to have faith in Canada. Many of these are the Indigenous people who are actually paid big salaries to have faith in Canada, or at least to pretend they do. The small group of elites have built careers in government-funded boards and organizations, and in these cases colonialism doesn't have to be overtly coercive. It can also co-opt an elite, which then brings the rest of the colonized society to the surrender table. This is what is often referred to as neocolonialism. It was no accident, for example, that Phil Fontaine, three-time elected leader of the Assembly of

First Nations, went on to become a highly paid consultant for Canadian banks, then an oil industry player and then turned up, literally, front and centre at the Trudeau victory celebration in October 2015. Now he is preparing to profit from the Liberal legalization of marijuana by setting up an "Indigenous" marijuana growing operation.

Phil is, in fact, the rule rather than the exception. The two other most recent AFN national chiefs, Ovide Mercredi and Shawn Atleo, have been named to the advisory board of Pacific Future Energy Corporation, an oil company with a plan to build a $12 billion oil refinery on the B.C. coast that will tanker processed bitumen to Asia. The nature of the company and the board is reflected in the chair, Stockwell Day, former Alberta PC cabinet member and leader of the Reform Party.

That is the system in Canada today, where Indigenous leaders who play the game are rewarded in fantastic ways, and we have a long list of our "leaders" taking this route to personal wealth.

We have spoken much about colonialism, but have not broached the idea of neocolonialism and how that works to undermine us at every turn. The term was first coined in Africa by the president of Ghana, Kwame Nkrumah, in the early 1960s, when he noticed that even though many African countries had won their independence, the colonial powers continued to exercise a stranglehold on the economy and politics of their countries. They accomplished this with the help of a small cadre of nationals who were well paid to ensure that, despite democratic reforms, real power remained with the former colonial masters.

This is the model we see in Canada with Indigenous people, and this neocolonial system has created deep political divisions between the grassroots and the Indigenous establishment.

The only way to address this problem is for the grassroots to use their vastly superior numbers and energy to challenge how decisions are being made on our land and in our communities.

I would like to make it clear that in most cases I am not speaking about direct challenges to the local Indian Act band chiefs, who have, in fact, very limited powers. In my father's time, band affairs were directly under the thumb of the superintendent of the Department of Indian Affairs. He fought to have the chiefs and councils recognized as leaders because we needed some kind of recognized leadership. He fought all his life for this, but in the end he told me that he felt control had been taken over by the band administrator. And band administrators are actually under the thumb of the Department of Indian Affairs, because that is where their power comes from, from the money allocated to them from federal government financial contributions. The chiefs themselves were largely irrelevant in the political struggle.

That is an unfortunate fact. But in the struggle to decolonize we should not waste our time and energy fighting against Indian Act chiefs. As an elected chief — which I was for eight years — you are aware that when you take over the government-created programs and services you also assume the financial responsibilities that come with them. From experience, I can tell you that funding comes with fundamental limits on what you can say and do. These are inhibitions that gradually take over the scope and depth of your actions, even though you are not really aware of it until you have again stepped outside the box. Then you see how profoundly inhibiting those government-funded Indian Act positions really are.

So we should focus instead much more broadly on the decolonial struggle. The chiefs, in the great majority of cases, will not lead (with some very notable exceptions in my experience — among them the Secwepemc chiefs Judy Wilson and Ryan Day, a number of the Algonquin chiefs and a few others around the country), because for the most part, that is not their role. They are paid to administer Indian Affairs programs and services. In this struggle, it is the grassroots people who must lead, and eventually our Indian Act chiefs will follow.

Much more problematic for us are those who are sometimes described as hang-around-the-fort Indians, a whole class of Native leaders working in off-reserve organizations funded almost exclusively by the government of Canada, and who have been negotiating almost continuously since the late 1980s on the government terms of surrender. Many have built lucrative careers on this and have been rewarded with Canadian honours, but they have not won any substantial victories for our people on the fundamental issues arising from our legally recognized rights.

These "leaders" and their paid consultants have also done enormous damage to our political and economic position with backroom deals that sell our resources — often for ridiculously low prices, which they often end up pocketing as wages and commissions. In one case I know of, mining rights to Aboriginal title lands were sold for a one-time $30,000 payment — the equivalent of less than a year's pension for a single retired bus driver in Burnaby — to compensate a community of five hundred people in perpetuity for absconding with their mineral wealth and polluting their land. These government-paid representatives are helping to perpetuate the neocolonialist system that entraps us.

We cannot avoid clashing with them when our sovereignty as well as our resources are being sold off.

Once they retire from the government-funded organizations, many of these "leaders" acquire lucrative "consulting" jobs. The great majority of these have also gravitated toward the Liberal honeypot. That is how the great neocolonial game works. The only problem is that our neocolonial leadership is playing the game with chips they do not own — the sovereignty and the territorial integrity of their people and their traditional lands.

STEALING FROM THE POOR

The emergence of support behind the Idle No More movement is precisely because of its grassroots nature. Young people especially are dissatisfied with the lack of success of our establishment organizations, like the First Nations Summit and Assembly of First Nations. They see the band administration or establishment as part of the problem and not the solution. And today they are trying to build new Indigenous alternative structures that will lead our decolonization battle.

In addressing these issues, we cannot simply stay on the sidelines, or merely focus on criticizing individuals. We have to look at the bigger underlying problems of how government funding is used to exercise control over who we elect to our leadership at all levels. Once again, we have to look at how our poverty is both a symptom of our oppression and a tool that is used to prolong it.

In many cases, our people are worried about making sure the band is in the good books of Indigenous and Northern Affairs, because members of their family depend on the welfare money coming from Canada. That is the reality of being poor, regardless if that poverty is because of lack of skills, bad luck or is systematically created by colonial relationships between settlers and Indigenous peoples. Poverty is an overpowering and crushing reality that keeps you perpetually mired in the moment, worrying about your responsibility as mom and dad to provide food, clothing and shelter to those you are responsible for, living hand-to-mouth on a monthly, weekly, daily or hourly basis. Canadian law-makers know this, and prefer Indigenous peoples to be poor because it is much easier to steal from poor people — who are almost completely defenceless — than rich people. You see this every day around us, not only in Canada but in the wider world. Five years ago, Oxfam reported that twenty-two individuals had the same amount of wealth as 50 per cent of the population of the world — that is 3.5 billion people. Today it is down to six individuals who have the same wealth as 3.5 billion people. You can get very rich from stealing from the poor because we are so numerous. You do not need to be Einstein to figure that out. In our case, the Creator gave us land that is rich enough that poverty is a result of our oppression. It is the existing federal and provincial resource allocation system that ensures our perpetual poverty.

The sad fact is, the Canadian government is using our poverty against us and our leadership is assisting them. That is why we the people have to step outside the government system and demand real change from grassroots, anti-colonial organizations that do not accept any funding from the government. That is where our leadership must come from today. It cannot come from inside the system, because the system simply won't allow it.

CHAPTER 17

WHERE HAVE THE LEADERS GONE?

The recent government moves to "reconcile" our title and rights to Canada's needs and desires are yet another attempt to orchestrate us into oblivion. Yet our organizations are nowhere to be seen in this battle that is essential to our future.

In fact, they seem to be vaguely nodding their approval to government attacks on our rights. It is ridiculous to interpret Section 35, which says that the federal and provincial government recognize and affirm existing Aboriginal and treaty rights, to mean we must reconcile those rights out of existence, subsuming them within federal and provincial government powers. Section 35 is in the Constitution to protect our Aboriginal and treaty rights. That is why it was put there and that is what is says. But the new government interpretation of the Supreme Court of Canada decisions is that Section 35 means that we are supposed to give up our Aboriginal rights to validate Canada, and we must agree that, according to their "legal reconciliation technique," our Section 35 rights cannot override the modern treaty.

I have not heard any of our establishment organizations speak out against this policy, which remains the policy of the Trudeau government's Indigenous and Northern Affairs. Forty years ago, they would not have considered even suggesting that kind of genocidal policy for Indigenous peoples. My father told me that we need to be very careful about getting a white man's education, because after you get it you need to retrain yourself back into your Indigenous thinking. Our leadership seems to have absorbed not only white man's learning but their values as well. And in the process they have forgotten who they are.

We cannot let the government-paid leadership or even the chiefs decide on the future of our land. People must have a direct voice and they must let the chiefs know that they cannot deal away our future behind closed doors.

I saw this in my own nation. I was invited as an observer to a meeting at Adams Lake, the neighbouring reserve to Neskonlith, between the chiefs and the government's Major Projects Management Office, headed by the assistant deputy minister. Government officials droned on with elaborate promises of advantages to come if we signed away our rights, and the atmosphere in the room was almost unbearable. Then the Secwepemc women, who were very unhappy about this closed meeting between government and government-paid chiefs, arrived singing traditional songs. They immediately kicked out the assistant deputy minister and the Major Projects Management people. Then they convinced the chiefs to sit down and have a community meeting with them so we could sort of regroup and talk about things collectively.

This is what we have to do as nations before we even think of discussing our future with the government. We must have honest discussions amongst ourselves, where Elders and youth and the women of the nation are present and actively consulted, for they are the title holders of the land and not a handful of hand-picked Indian Act chiefs and councillors.

The establishment organizations like the Assembly of First Nations have also shifted away from where their people are actually living. The level of poverty and hopelessness in my community, for example, is not addressed by the legislation, programs and services that are being offered them. Nothing that is being offered addresses their hopelessness. They are being told to hoist themselves up by their own bootstraps by people who have not even noticed that today they have no bootstraps. Our bootstraps are our Aboriginal title lands and our right to self-determination. If our leadership would focus on winning recognition for both of these items we would as peoples be off and running without any further help.

But unfortunately, Indian organizations are led and staffed by an Indian elite who have used our people's poverty to leverage their own government-funded jobs. In their eagerness to please the ones who are paying them, they have forgotten about the people who they are supposed to be serving. Our leaders have abandoned our people and many of them have simply boarded the Trudeau train and disappeared from Indian country into cushy jobs in Ottawa. They are no longer hanging around the Liberal fort, they have disappeared into it.

SELF-INJURY

As co-chair of the AFN Delgamuukw Implementation Strategic Committee, I contacted Indian Affairs Minister Robert Nault to ask if, in the wake of the Supreme Court's landmark Delgamuukw decision, he was going to review the extinguishment policy. He shook his head. There was no need, he said, because so many Indian bands were still negotiating under it. Since the government policy was not going to be reviewed, he said that my community should also consider joining negotiations, because the policy was actually quite flexible — which of course it is not. In fact, the only exit from those negotiations is through extinguishment of Aboriginal title and rights.

Many grassroots Indigenous people do not know that their participation in these treaty negotiations actually hurts them. It sometimes seems that those who are negotiating cannot stop because they are dependent upon the money they get through treaty loans from the federal and provincial governments. But continuing at these termination tables is the single greatest injury that we inflict on ourselves and our future. In fact, if we are to have a future at all, we must walk away from these termination tables and refuse to come back until the government agrees to recognize our Section 35 rights and to address us as nations. It is as simple and as difficult as that.

CHAPTER 18

AROUND THE MULBERRY BUSH

My friend Russell Diabo and I have the same discussion at least once a year. Along with being one of the most important Indigenous political analysts in North America and publisher of the First Nations Strategic Bulletin, Russell works as an advisor for the Algonquin Nation in dealing with the issues that come flying at them on a daily basis.

His feelings about the dismal performance of the Assembly of First Nations in protecting our rights are as strong, or even stronger, than my own, but he feels he has to at least try to influence the organization — nudging it toward defending our rights or at least away from the cliff edge — even if this is generally a lost cause. I am always skeptical about this but, in fact, I can't fault his reasoning.

"If we don't try to influence what happens at the AFN," he says, "the First Nation communities we work with will be affected whether we like it or not."

We recently discussed whether we should put energy into trying to get the AFN to elevate itself above getting money from Canada, to fighting for our rights under the UN human rights treaties.

We were not hopeful that the AFN was capable of this. The problem is the lack of capacity of most of the elected chiefs to think at that level, because their entire political discourse is based on holding onto and, if possible, expanding band funding programs from Ottawa. And nothing would make the giving hand withdraw faster than asking that our internationally recognized right to self-determination be respected.

The question was, could we push the chiefs' thinking beyond getting cheques from Ottawa to fighting for our human rights under international treaties.

Those are two very different worlds. Poor people are always on the edge of calamity and most chiefs are so busy managing our poverty they have no time to even reflect on how that poverty was created in the first place. When you are forced to live life on the ledge, you don't ask how you got there. You are too busy making sure that you don't slip and fall.

On those rare occasions that the AFN, which is in every way a chief's organization, addresses the issue of self-determination, they go hat in hand to Ottawa to ask for self-determination in the same way as they ask for program funding — start out demanding a lot but happy if in the end they get a little. This is, I have to say, demented.

Self-determination is not something you can ask someone to give you, like funding for a water treatment plant. You either have it or you don't. Self-determination is an international remedy to colonization. It is not a domestic institution to be determined by the colonial state government — especially the government that is imposing and benefiting from colonial entitlements of 100 per cent control over Indigenous peoples' territories.

The only argument that the AFN uses in favour of our self-determination is one that tries to play on guilt — be nice to us now because you were mean to us in the past. From a negotiating point of view, it is impossible to move a body that is benefiting from your land from a position of guilt. When you stand pathetically, hat in hand, and ask meekly for your country back, the best that you can hope for is a sympathetic hug (the Liberal approach) before being sent on your way. Like Einstein said, insanity is doing the same thing over and over again and expecting different results. That is the problem of domesticated thinking about our right to self-determination. It is not something to be given to us by the government, but something that we have and must exercise to the fullest.

The bodies most capable of dealing with our right to self-determination are the UN human rights bodies responsible for seeing that Canada is implementing Article 1 of the International Covenant on Civil and Political Rights (ICCPR) and the International Covenant on Economic, Social and Cultural Rights (ICESCR). It is to the international organizations that our leaders have to go to demand that our right to self-determination is recognized by the settler-state government and incorporated into the Canadian Constitution. Right now, the settler-state government is enjoying self-determination at our expense and this is reflected in the systemic poverty we experience on a day-to-day basis. The international organizations understand this. When Canada tells them what wonderful and enlightened treatment Indigenous peoples receive in Canada, the international experts always ask the same question: why, then, are Indigenous peoples still so poor?

They understand that poverty is not a consequence of our land being poor; it is because the colonial system we live under systemically impoverishes us by preventing us from using our land.

International work allows fresh air into the room. Indigenous peoples need to understand that Aboriginal law as it is practised in this country is basically colonial law, so their rights are always, ultimately, overlooked or intentionally obscured. The problem is that our existing leadership doesn't seem to understand this.

So once again, my friend Russell Diabo drafts a resolution that calls on the leadership to confront the government from a position of strength in demanding that it respects our inalienable right to self-determination and our inherent right to self-government. One of a handful of sympathetic chiefs puts it before the AFN general assembly. We suspect that it will get overwhelming support from the floor and it will be duly noted in the resolution book, but nothing will be done about it. The leadership of the AFN, whose salaries are paid by Canada, do not want to embarrass Canada on the world stage. And the issue of our fundamental right to self-determination is one issue the AFN cannot address at the negotiating tables with the government because they are dependent on government money. No government will pay us to talk about our right to self-determination. They only pay our people who agree to talk about our surrender.

This is ironic because, while our own Indigenous leadership runs and hides from this issue, I find that in the meetings I hold in university classrooms, church basements and even legion halls across the land more and more non-Indigenous Canadians are beginning to get it. This is especially true from so-called "visible minorities," blacks and Asians and other people of colour who don't need to be told how Canada actually works. They understand the workings of colonialism instinctively and many of these minorities, and recently a growing number of white Canadians, come up to me after meetings to say, okay, what is to be done? How do we get rid of colonialism and how do we live together afterward?

I tell them the answer is simple. Canada needs to fully recognize our Aboriginal and treaty rights and our absolute right to self-determination. At the same time, we will recognize the fundamental human right of Canadians, after hundreds of years of settlement, to live here. Then we can sit down and negotiate a way that Canadians and Indigenous peoples can live on this vast shared land in a way that allows for prosperity for both societies and protects our environment for all of the generations to come. (This is something we will explore in more detail in the final section.)

Non-Indigenous Canadians in ever-greater numbers understand this. But much of our leadership is still too timid to put even this basic position forward. This allows the governments, with the help of the neocolonial forces in our community that they finance, to fight its determined rearguard action against us and against justice for Indigenous peoples.

This, in fact, is how it unfolded. The AFN voted on Russell's motion. As expected, it was overwhelmingly supported by the chiefs. And then it disappeared into that dark void where, for many decades now, progressive AFN resolutions go to die.

FIGHTING ASSIMILATION

In my father's time it was clear. There was the Indian community and there was the Department of Indian Affairs, with a clear distinction between the two groups. That does not exist anymore in Indigenous communities in Canada because too many of them have accepted federal government policies. The line of opposition is no longer between Indians and the Department of Indian Affairs, but inside our communities themselves.

You cannot deal in a spirit of cooperation and kindness with a system designed to steal everything from you and destroy you. The grassroots need to know that we have to be very cautious of the processes we get involved in and we need to keep our distance from dragging the government policy lines into our band offices and organizations.

Once you accept government policy and accept to administer government programs and services, you become government — clear and simple. People do not yet understand that. When they do, they will once again be able to fight together with force and clarity, instead of the unhappy position we find ourselves in today when we must fight against one another.

This is complicated by the fact that our establishment organizations have disappeared so far down the path of our termination that it seems they can no longer find their way back to the grassroots people and their needs. Many chiefs have even borrowed money from the government — in B.C. a total of more than $500 million that the small impoverished communities will one day have to pay back — in order to negotiate away their people's Aboriginal title and rights at government-controlled negotiation tables.

What does it say about our establishment organizations that they themselves get millions of dollars per year from dependency agencies in Ottawa and provincial capitals? Funding is the issue, and it is something we avoid talking about. I come from the generation that saw the first money come in from the government. It was my dad's generation that took that money. They debated about it back then and finally decided to take the money. I think we need to debate it again.

When you selflessly participate in the struggle, it means doing this kind of work without pay. I have been basically unemployed since 1988. I work on this issue on a daily basis, but I do not get paid from any source. That is why I can say what I say — I am broke but I am free. Indigenous peoples need to know that freedom does, indeed, have a price. Settlers will not suddenly give us freedom. No, they are going to throw us in jail when we decide to demand our freedom from their colonialist system. Millions of white people are spending our money right now. We will have to fight to get it back or be satisfied with welfare. The colonialists will only fund a small group of Indigenous peoples to act as neocolonial managers — that's all. For the rest of us, it is sink or swim, even if that means swimming, as we do now, against the tide but toward justice.

Funding is directly linked to plugging into the charity programs of federal and provincial governments or plugging into the capitalist economies of the federal and provincial governments. You have no self-determination under those economic arrangements. None of your values are listened to or reflected through federal and provincial government legislation, regulation and policies. We are still just a fairly meaningless add-on expense under the fairly meaningless legal "duty to consult" with Indigenous peoples.

I have never seen a real duty to consult policy or process that builds up our economic power. They are merely procedures to agree to economic plans put forward by the settlers, because Indigenous peoples normally do not have the money to invest in our own land nor do we know the process by which we can borrow the money to do so.

The AFN is merely playing along. We need to create the situation where Canadians and the international community begin to question the very colonial system under which we are living and see that we must fundamentally change it in a way that takes into account the basic human rights of Indigenous peoples. The AFN and the establishment leaders have to decide to walk with us and if they cannot, they should get out of our way.

CHAPTER 19

THE GRASSROOTS STRUGGLE: DEFENDERS OF THE LAND AND IDLE NO MORE

The federal and provincial governments have tens of millions of dollars that they use strategically to manipulate Indigenous organizations and to undermine the grassroots from moving forward. One of their strategies in B.C. is to "engage" Indigenous leadership in all kinds of negotiations that go nowhere. Modern treaty negotiations have been happening for twenty-one years now and cost well over a billion dollars. While they are negotiating, they can at least pretend to investors that everything is under control. The Indians are at the negotiating table and eventually they will agree to the government's extinguishment terms. So the "uncertainty" is only temporary.

The Indigenous leadership and their non-Indigenous advisors involved in these negotiations justify sitting down with the government because, they say, "only by holding discussions with the government can we make change." They see those of us who will not negotiate under the government's terms as frozen in time, of not being capable of moving forward, of not getting with the program. Needless to say, the governments agree with the leadership and welcome them with open arms. They know they are a soft group to deal with, because they have already agreed, by sitting down at the table, that their people's own extinguishment will be the basis of the land claims agreement they will eventually sign.

Part of the reason for this is that our mainstream organizations generally select our leadership on the basis of money. They know that government money will quickly dry up if they elect leaders who fight for decolonization, but a compliant leadership attracts government money like horse dung attracts flies. People in Indigenous leadership know this and there is an unwritten blacklist of people who will be excluded from the organizations because they are too grassroots. They only work with people who are acceptable to government.

It is this underlying reality that has given rise to the Defenders of the Land. Those who cannot accept the fact that chiefs and councils will not rock the boat because they want to protect their government funding have no alternative but to work outside the mainstream organizations.

At the same time, Defenders have to recognize that part of those funds are also necessary for many of our band members — our grassroots — who in our dismal state of dependency cannot afford to have their programs and services cut off. If we are going to do things that will threaten their lifelines, they need to be part of the decision-making process. We must try to ensure that we do not put our people in an impossible situation, and we do this by working outside of the chiefs and council band structure but always working closely with the grassroots.

In this way, the Defenders and Idle No More are the basis for building a movement in Canada. No one else will play this role except us and we can build on the considerable discontent floating around in communities. Even with the Trudeau charm offensive, people see that things are not adding up. One thing is promised but another is delivered.

We have seen again and again that the prime minister and premiers are not interested in giving up one inch of power to Indigenous peoples, and Prime Minister Justin Trudeau is no exception. You are daydreaming if you think you can negotiate your way to freedom without creating tension to push our colonizers to decolonize Canada.

Our only advantage in this fight is that our communities are spread across Canada in over a thousand locations, and they cannot take us all on at once. But unless we forcefully demand our rights, including our fundamental right to self-determination, we will not receive them. As minorities everywhere and in all times know, that is how the world works. And that is what our current leadership, generally for their own self-serving reasons, is refusing to acknowledge.

This is why Idle No More and Defenders of the Land were formed. They reject not only the government's colonial policies, but those in our leadership who cooperate with the government's colonialist policies. We are working to re-establish grassroots organizations, strategies and actions that will get us back on the road to defending our sovereignty and our ownership of our lands. Our people are fighting now at the grassroots level to achieve self-determination, free from the colonial state.

We see courageous Indigenous people doing this every day, and if we cannot join them in these actions, we should at least support them in every way that we can. They are the future of our struggle and our struggle is building a new, decolonized Canada, where our cultures and land rights are respected.

DEPENDENCY PROGRAMS

In accepting the dependency programs and services offered to us by Canada and administered at our band offices, we are playing into the colonial strategy that begins with the dispossession of our land and continues by creating our absolute dependency on the colonial state. We need to be able to connect the dots between dispossession, dependency, economic exploitation and oppression.

Decolonization, self-determination and economic independence are the key ingredients of our struggle as Indigenous peoples. But the Canadian government is attempting to tie the colonial knot tighter and tighter around our establishment organizations — to make the Assembly of First Nations, provincial and territorial organizations, tribal councils and chief and councils nothing more than Indian branch offices to the dependency mechanism of Indigenous and Northern Affairs.

The termination policy is basically the final step in the colonization of Indigenous peoples. It makes our dispossession complete by constitutionally and legally breaking our connection to our lands. The termination policy was expressed by Canada in the *Statement of the Government of Canada on Indian Policy*, also known as the 1969 White Paper, and through existing government strategies to terminate our rights. The termination policy is like segregation in the US and apartheid in South Africa. It must be defeated if we are to have a future as Indigenous peoples. We need to take examples from men like Nelson Mandela and Martin Luther King, Jr.

Nelson Mandela was a great man because he gave up his personal freedom to fight against apartheid. He could have walked out of prison much earlier than the twenty-seven years he spent there if he had been willing to accept apartheid — or at least promise not to fight against it. He refused and it took twenty-seven years before the white South African governments had to admit that apartheid was wrong and move to change it. And please note that reconciliation did not happen until after apartheid was off the table. Mr. Mandela stood on principle. Our leaders must also stand on principle because our issues are also based on the human and Indigenous rights of our peoples.

We should stop negotiating with any government that does not recognize our Aboriginal and treaty rights. We should stop negotiating with the governments to take over the dependency programs and services unless our Aboriginal and treaty rights are recognized and affirmed, so we can build an independent economic base for our people. We should stop negotiating under any policy that does not recognize and affirm our Aboriginal and treaty rights first. We should take example from Nelson Mandela that we will not negotiate with the governments if "termination" is still on the table, like Nelson Mandela refused to negotiate if "apartheid" was still on the table.

I know a lot of establishment leaders do not like walking away from the negotiating table unless there is some kind of alternative. They have to know that it is up to us to create our alternative by mobilizing the grassroots and demanding decolonization at the international level. No peoples have ever been given a well-groomed path to liberation. That is something you must be willing to make with your own sweat and tears.

CHAPTER 20
UNITY AROUND
A STRONG POSITION

Our goal today has to be building a critical mass around a strong position. The focus must be on the Defenders of the Land and Idle No More, both of which are free of government funding and free to push for our right to self-determination.

When I see the trouble we are in with those who have sold out their ideals and their people for government-funded careers, I know now that we should have been stronger in taking them on in the 1975–90 period. I remember my brother Bobby, who was band chief during this period and came within one vote from being elected national chief in 1980, talking about a pendulum. He said that the deal makers of the day — Joe Mathias, George Watts and Bill Wilson, who broke away from the Union of B.C. Indian Chiefs in the late 1970s — were getting support from some communities because, like Donald Trump today, they boasted about their superior deal-making skills in getting all that we needed from governments. Bobby said that support would swing back to us when people saw that their way did not work. Today it is obvious that these vaunted "deal makers" have left us in a weaker position than when the Union was powered by a peoples movement and actually managed to effect change by forcing the inclusion of Section 35 in the Constitution.

What it will take to bring the more principled solution all the way back is hope, courage and perseverance on our part. When I talk about these things, I am not using the flowery expressions of speech makers, I am talking about real emotions that we need to feel and express if we are going to move forward in the spirit of the Defenders of the Land and Idle No More. It is through hope, courage and perseverance that we can break away from our existing government-funded leadership and become a thoroughly grassroots movement united around the position of our internationally recognized right to self-determination. As long as recognition and affirmation of Aboriginal and treaty rights rests only domestically — in Ottawa and the provinces and in the colonial courts — we are in trouble. We must fight as people of the Fourth World, the Indigenous peoples of the world whose population the UN has estimated at 370 million — together we would be the third largest country in the world after China and India.

I believe the framework is in place. What we need is the courage and the tenacity to become real nations, and we have to begin by standing united, taking what may come.

Our actions have to start at the community level, fighting the land battles and our fights for our land rights, and, as we assert our right to self-determination, these battles can take us all the way to Geneva and New York City — as we will examine in the next section.

Idle No More and the Defenders of the Land are the ideal grassroots driving force of this movement. The pendulum, as we saw with the Idle No More uprising of the winter of 2012–13, is swinging our way. Now more than ever we have to dedicate ourselves to work with hope, courage and perseverance to mobilize the grassroots people, the real rights holders, to claim back what is rightfully theirs. It remains a battle on many fronts — constitutional, legal and political, as well as on the ground and internationally — and we must actively pursue all of them at the same time.

CONNECTING THE DOTS

So this is where we are today.

Indigenous peoples and the Indigenous leadership need to connect the dots from the local to the international in order to achieve justice. We need to understand that the fundamental issue is our land and the natural wealth that it produces. Our biggest strength is in the economic uncertainty that our legal, constitutional and political actions create for the status quo. Canada and the provinces have gotten used to the colonial privilege of having the final say on resource development in our Aboriginal and treaty territories. That is why Indigenous peoples need to expect stiff opposition when we fight against the economic exploitation of our impoverished grassroots.

We want to begin serious negotiations with the government, but we cannot have reconciliation until the termination policy is off the table and our Aboriginal and treaty rights are recognized, affirmed and implemented by Canada and the provinces — recognized and affirmed not only in the Constitution, but on the ground. We need to negotiate for results, not money to keep a negotiation process going that produces nothing except more debt and dependency. It is not disrespectful to talk about collaborators as being counter-productive to our human rights. We need to stand up and fight colonialism in all its manifestations. We need to root out the racism and impoverishment that colonialism systematically creates for the vast majority of our peoples.

The Creator did not give the settlers the right to exclusively benefit from our natural wealth and resources. It is colonialism, and now neocolonialism and its racist legal processes, that gives the settlers the power to economically exploit us as Indigenous peoples.

It is our responsibility to move Canada beyond exploitation and help the global community move one step closer to peace and security for all.

We have international law on our side. At the core of our struggle today is the demand that all of our international rights contained in the UN Declaration of the Rights of Indigenous Peoples be respected by governments in Canada. We will not accept a pick-and-choose approach by the government or half measures. Those are our rights; all forty-six of the articles must be respected.

The Trudeau government may try to say, as it did in 2016, that it is the "painful truth" that the UN Declaration of the Rights of Indigenous Peoples cannot be adopted by Canada "word for word" but only in some sanitized Canadian form. But in this they are once again playing cynical word games. UNDRIP is an international treaty that was twenty years in the making — the Canadian parliament cannot simply unilaterally amend it. You either adopt it or not. You either respect it or you abrogate it. You cannot call transgressions "amendments." They are simply transgressions and we must fight to have the letter of the law obeyed in Canada. If our government-paid leadership refuses to fight, the grassroots must fight both in Canada and internationally. That is the battle ground we will look at now.

PART 5
THE FAMILY OF NATIONS

CHAPTER 21

THE INTERNATIONAL STAGE

Stephen Harper left us with a sense that he was completely tuned out about the United Nations. His international obsessions seemed to include Ukraine, where Putin was to blame, and Israel, where the Palestinians were to blame. It was black and white and the rest of the world, apart from Washington, seemed to be viewed as a shapeless grey mass of no potential interest for Canada.

Justin Trudeau, on the other hand, seems eager to win the approval of the United Nations, most notably in getting back for Canada a seat on the Security Council, which it was denied for the first time under the Harper regime. Trudeau began lobbying for this shortly after taking office, when he hosted UN Secretary-General Ban Ki-moon in Ottawa with full head of state honours.

But Canada's human rights record was damaged not only by Harper's indifference toward the non-Ukrainian and non-Israeli foreigners at the UN, but also by its continued failures to live up to its commitments regarding the human and specifically Indigenous rights of the Indigenous peoples within its borders. And we must continue to make this a major issue at United Nations gatherings.

We need to show, at the international level, why Canada and countries with Indigenous peoples within their borders need international management. Because when it is challenged, the colonial state tends to resort to violence in order to maintain the status quo. In the case of Canada, the federal and provincial governments frequently use their police forces, and at times even the army, to physically force Indigenous peoples to comply with colonial laws — despite the fact they have competing and internationally recognized legal rights to the same territory.

We have labelled this process "criminalization" of Indigenous activists. In fact, the Defenders of the Land have been researching its effects and have assembled a list of the hundreds of Indigenous people in Canada who have been violated this way — and I do mean hundreds. This includes several members of my immediate and extended family.

In the face of this repression, we need a broader vision of how we will achieve decolonization and self-determination. One of the primary steps is to make Canadians aware of their government's human rights violations toward Indigenous peoples.

Our struggle is just as significant and politically complicated as desegregation in the southern US or getting rid of apartheid in South Africa. Both these struggles required international attention to force the status quo to change. Our struggle will also need international support, and this is something we have to begin to build now. We cannot be shy about taking Canada on in front of the eyes of the world as a human rights abuser.

THE FOURTH WORLD

My father was always working to achieve self-determination for Indigenous peoples at the international level and it was he who coined the term the "fourth world," which describes our situation as the legitimate owners of our Indigenous territories while our lands are being occupied and controlled by settler societies. He felt that, despite this complicated situation, we could not be denied a remedy. And the remedy against colonial oppression is the right to self-determination.

One of Canada's secret fears is that once our right to self-determination is recognized, Indigenous peoples would be able to separate from Canada — in the way that Quebec separatists have been trying to do for the past fifty years. This is based on fear that under respective UN declarations and provisions for decolonization, colonized or dependent peoples ultimately achieve independence from their colonial masters. Canada will not, of course, even consider that as a possibility.

My father understood this, and that is why he wanted to make a distinction between decolonization of the third world and decolonization of Indigenous peoples in the fourth world. Our nations have been swamped by the settler societies and all we are asking is that our land rights and our right to self-determination be respected within that space. Self-determination in this context means the absolute right for, say, the Secwepemc people to live their lives as Secwepemc — with the means to live on our own land and build a sustainable economic life and a culture that allows us to revive our language and follow our own customs within the Canadian space. All this can be achieved in a respectful manner — where we respect Canadians' needs and they respect ours.

That is the message that my own people have been taking to Ottawa for more than a century. But federal and provincial governments throw up their hands and tell us this is not even conceivable. Meanwhile, a small province like Prince Edward Island with 143,000 people has, like all provinces, complete control of their lands, resources, and health, justice, agricultural and transportation systems, as well as their own fully funded health care and primary, secondary and post-secondary education systems — thanks to transfer payments. But these simple constitutional rights, which strengthen Canada, are said to be inconceivable for the million or so Indigenous peoples in the country.

It is because of this intransigence that we have been forced to take our struggle to the world. And this is not new. There is a long tradition of Indigenous peoples from Canada seeking justice outside Canada's borders. Just among the Secwepemc people in British Columbia, my great uncle, Chief William Parrish from Neskonlith, went to London in 1926 to protest the non-recognition and implementation of their land rights by the colonial government. As mentioned, my father, Grand Chief George Manuel, founded the first international Indigenous organization, the World Council of Indigenous Peoples (WCIP) in 1975, which has been recognized by many contemporary international leaders as a precursor to the present international Indigenous institutions. Numerous Secwepemc people, including my father and brother, Bobby, travelled to European capitals during the Constitutional patriation debate.

I first travelled to Europe in 1999 to appear before the UN Working Group on Indigenous Populations as Neskonlith band chief as well as the chairman of the Shuswap Nation Tribal Council, and I have been back lobbying in Europe on almost an annual basis since then. In 2005, the late Elder Irene Billy, accompanied by my son, Ska7cis, travelled to Geneva to raise land rights issues, including the expansion of Sun Peaks Resort without the prior informed consent of Secwepemc people. Secwepemc leaders were also organizers of UN Special Rapporteur Rodolfo Stavenhagen's unofficial visit to Canada in 2003. Special Rapporteur Stavenhagen visited Sun Peaks Resort and met with other activist groups. Secwepemc people have been active in the North American Indigenous Peoples Caucus (NAIPC) at the UN Permanent Forum of Indigenous Issues, and I have co-chaired both the NAIPC and the International Indigenous Caucus. The Aboriginal Title Alliance, of which I am a member through my band, has also submitted reports to UN Special Rapporteurs James Anaya and Victoria Tauli-Corpuz.

These examples of international battles are just from the Secwepemc nation — a nation of ten thousand people in the B.C. Interior. But virtually all of the sixty Indigenous nations in Canada have sent representatives abroad at one time or another seeking justice in the international sphere. Today it is time that we go together to ask the world to support us in our decolonization quest. Indigenous peoples in Canada have always looked to the international community for justice when we cannot get justice here in Canada. It is time we took our case to the world in full force, with representatives of the sixty nations in Canada speaking in one voice, demanding self-determination and decolonization.

CHAPTER 22

CONSTITUTIONAL DEADLOCK AND THE INTERNATIONAL OPTION

It was during the 1982 patriation of the Canadian Constitution that the question of the status of Indigenous nations in Canada became, undeniably, an international question. This was, in turn, a result of the vortex of activity in 1980 — protests throughout Canada, a massive protest in Ottawa, and Indigenous delegations sent to the United Nations, to the Russell Tribunal in The Hague and, most significantly, to Westminster in London to petition for the UK to block the patriation of the Constitution without the inclusion of a formal recognition of Aboriginal title and treaty rights.

As we know, those rights were included in Section 35 and, as we have already seen, the mechanism to actually define them was set out in Section 37: the series of high-level conferences by the three legal entities in Canada — the federal government, the provincial governments and the Indigenous peoples, who were represented by their national First Nations, Inuit and Métis organizations.

After four often bitter and acrimonious meetings between 1983 and 1987, the political class in Canada walked away from the process without any substantive progress being made. In effect, they were refusing to resolve the colonial relationship that existed between Canada and Indigenous peoples since Confederation in 1867.

But that did not mean the process was over. When rights of nations are at stake, one party cannot simply walk away and end the matter. When this is done, the petitioning party has the absolute right to seek other remedies. This means that Indigenous peoples had a right to address their land and self-governing issues not only under colonial courts, which by definition can offer only partial satisfaction, but under the United Nations protection for all peoples, particularly under Article 1 of the International Covenant on Civil and Political Rights, which asserts that "All peoples have the right to self-determination."

This claim of Indigenous protection under the International Covenant on Civil and Political Rights was confirmed by the passage by the United Nations General Assembly in 2007 of the Declaration on the Rights of Indigenous Peoples. It echoes the International Covenant with the assertion in Article 3 stating that "Indigenous peoples have the right to self-determination. By virtue of that right they freely determine their political status and freely pursue their economic, social and cultural development."

When Canada turned its back on the decolonial process by unilaterally ending the constitutionally mandated conferences in 1987, it left Indigenous peoples without a domestic resolution to their demands for self-government. It is clear that unrest among Indigenous peoples today, and grassroots movements like Idle No More, are intimately linked to the failure of Canada to decolonize its relationship with the

Indigenous peoples within its borders.

While we prepare to defy the government colonialists on the ground, we must also link with allies internationally to fight for that basic right to self determination that all peoples of the world possess as a birthright.

We will find a hearing there. The world is already well aware that there is something very wrong in Canada's treatment of the Indigenous peoples within its borders. The UN Special Rapporteur on the Rights of Indigenous Peoples has reported to the UN General Assembly that there is persistent disparity between Indigenous peoples and other Canadians, and Indigenous peoples are impoverished because the government has seized all of their lands and resources. This is where we must carry on with the fight today. We must hold Canada to the promises they made to the world when they signed the human rights treaties and covenants. They cannot respect the human rights of some and not others.

CHAPTER 23

WHAT THE UN SAYS ABOUT SELF-DETERMINATION

The moment you colonize a people, the moment you dispossess them of their lands and make them dependent, you create an urge to be free and an urge to be independent — the colonized will inevitably fight for these things and this will make true peace impossible. That is why the United Nations condemns all forms of colonialism — because colonialism is, at the most basic level, the enemy of peace.

It was no accident that the United Nations began to confront the fundamental injustices of colonialism shortly after its founding in the middle of the fiery cauldron of World War II, where small nations had been crushed and murderous racial policies had been unleashed against whole peoples. One of the first acts of the newly formed United Nations after the war was to proclaim the Universal Declaration of Human Rights. One of the lead drafters of that document was a Canadian professor, John Humphrey. One of the leading international figures who pushed for the declaration was Eleanor Roosevelt, who called the declaration "the international Magna Carta of all humankind." Nation states agreed to make this declaration a cornerstone

International Covenant on Civil and Political Rights

1966

Article 1

2. All peoples may, for their own ends, freely dispose of their natural wealth and resources without prejudice to any obligations arising out of international economic co-operation, based upon the principle of mutual benefit, and international law. In no case may a people be deprived of its own means of subsistence.

16-04-29

of international law by agreeing to nine basic human rights treaties to protect the rights of all nations. Canada was one of the first signatories to all of these treaties.

Three of the treaties directly impact Indigenous peoples, and the most important one is the International Covenant on Civil and Political Rights. Article 1 of the covenant says that all peoples are entitled to self-determination — to have the right to our territory, to be self sufficient, to have the right to govern ourselves under our own laws. Here is what the United Nations recognizes as the rights of all "peoples":

> Article 1 ICCPR and ICESCR — the right to self-determination
> All peoples have the right of self-determination. By virtue of that right they freely determine

their political status and freely pursue their economic, social and cultural development. All peoples may, for their own ends, freely dispose of their natural wealth and resources without prejudice to any obligations arising out of international economic co-operation, based upon the principle of mutual benefit, and international law. In no case may a people be deprived of its own means of subsistence. The States Parties to the present Covenant, including those having responsibility for the administration of Non-Self-Governing and Trust Territories, shall promote the realization of the right of self-determination, and shall respect that right, in conformity with the provisions of the Charter of the United Nations.

The establishment of Article 1 in Canada can only be achieved if the provisions of self-determination are mutually agreed between settlers and Indigenous peoples. That is the price settlers must pay when moving onto someone else's territory. The full application of Article 1 in Canada cannot be a unilateral decision made by the settler governments. This is the essence between how Article 1 in the International Covenant on Civil and Political Rights interacts with Article 3 of the United Nations Declaration on the Rights of Indigenous Peoples.

Canada's exercising of its own right to self-determination and assumption of Crown sovereignty (as referred to by the Supreme Court of Canada) is deeply entangled with pre-existing Aboriginal sovereignties and the initial colonial relationship Indigenous peoples had with the British Crown. The United Nations General Assembly passed Resolution 1514 in 1960, in which they clearly identified colonialism as a violation of the human rights of those being made dependent on the colonial state. The United Nations declared:

> 1. The subjection of peoples to alien subjugation, domination and exploitation constitutes a denial of fundamental human rights, is contrary to the Charter of the United Nations and is an impediment to the promotion of world peace and co-operation.
>
> 2. All peoples have the right to self-determination; by virtue of that right they freely determine their political status and freely pursue their economic, social and cultural development.

It is important to point out at this level of the discussion that Indigenous people need to become fully aware of what the United Nations has done in terms of self-determination, simply because many of the problems we face domestically have already been thought through by the United Nations. What is evident is that Canada is not a fully decolonized state, because it has not resolved its claim to control the land over the objections of Indigenous peoples. Canada must have Indigenous peoples' consent on how Aboriginal and treaty territories form the foundation of Canada — this is clear not only according to international law but according to Section 37 of its own

Constitution. Decolonization in Canada must therefore be measured against Canada's capacity to implement constitutionally recognized and affirmed Aboriginal and treaty rights on the ground. This is not happening in Canada, and the United Nations Human Rights Committee is responsible to see that this is done.

It is apparent from these materials that if you need self-determination, then you are actually a dependent people now. But the resolution makes it clear that we are not talking about Indigenous peoples declaring their independence and separating from Canada. That has never been a part of our movement and it is not foreseen in the international mechanisms of decolonization.

All Canada has to do to start these negotiations is to recognize our Aboriginal title and rights that are also acknowledged in the 1982 version of their own Constitution. That's all — to begin to behave as a lawful state that respects its own Constitution and the international covenants it has bound itself to.

The Canadian Constitution already recognizes provinces as having complete control over lands, resources, education, health care and many other essential parts of our lives, and this in no way diminishes Canada. It adds to it with the fundamental flexibility that only federalism can offer. If Indigenous people lived in one area, we would be the sixth largest province by population in the country, and for us to control all of our lands, resources, education, health care and many other essentials would be no more disruptive to other Canadians than provincial control is. The fact that we are more widely dispersed does not prevent us — as Indigenous peoples — from exercising these same powers.

Similarly, the fact that we are trapped inside a settler state does not preclude us from self-determination, it merely makes it a bit more complicated to achieve. But it also makes it more necessary. The persistent poverty that Indigenous peoples have been enduring is proof that the existing system does not work. We have become beggars on our own land while settlers have developed a strong and independent government on our territory. It is time for us to demand the minimum that is guaranteed all peoples in the family of nations: the right to govern ourselves on our own territory.

The world has been demanding this from Canada for more than a decade. It was in 2005 that the United Nations Human Rights Committee most clearly criticized Canada's processes and policies that deal with Indigenous land rights, because they resulted in de facto extinguishment. This is how well the world knows Canada. After hearing reports of the continued use of "extinguishment" and its "modification" and "non-assertion" versions, the UN Human Rights Committee asked Canada to explain what they were doing to fulfill their obligations to Indigenous nations under Article 1 of the UN covenant that recognizes the right to self-determination of all peoples.

Canada's silence on this issue has been deafening. So it is up to us to make noise. As much noise as we possibly can until the Canadian people hear us and realize that their government is oppressing Indigenous peoples at home and sullying the country's reputation abroad.

CHAPTER 24

CANADA'S HUMAN RIGHTS TREATIES

There are many doors in New York and Geneva for Indigenous people to knock on. All of them know of the injustice that settler states like Canada continue to mete out to Indigenous peoples. It is important that we are aware of this — that we know we are not alone. In fact, we are an important part of the world, even in simple numbers, and it is essential that we take our place with world bodies to push for recognition of our rights.

Of the human rights treaties that Canada has signed, the ones that concern Indigenous peoples and Canadian people are: the International Convention on the Elimination of All Forms of Racial Discrimination in 1965, the International Covenant on Economic, Social and Cultural Rights in 1966 and the International Covenant on Civil and Political Rights in 1966. And, of course, the much more recent UN Declaration of the Rights of Indigenous Peoples, which we will look at in a separate chapter.

Within the United Nations, most human rights committees and councils are managed or funded through the Office of the High Commission on Human Rights that was set up in 1993, immediately after the Cold War ended. Human rights bodies are divided into those that monitor adherence to the UN charters and those that monitor adherence to UN treaties. The charter-based monitors include the Human Rights Council and the treaty-based organizations include the Human Rights Committee (CCPR), the Committee on Economic, Social and Cultural Rights (CESCR) and the Committee on the Elimination of Racial Discrimination (CERD).

When the Canadian government signed on to these initial human rights treaties and covenants, they promised to reform the country's laws and policies to comply with their provisions. They also promised to inform citizens about their legal rights, to ensure the laws are implemented and fairly adjudicated and, if there was a violation, individuals should be able to file complaints or lawsuits to obtain justice. Canada also agreed to report to the various international agencies, committees and councils at regular intervals — usually every five years — on human rights progress within Canada.

I have attended many of these sessions and I can tell you that while Canada downplays the importance of the international procedures for its domestic audience, it takes the process very seriously. It shows up in Geneva, where most of the human rights agency and council meetings are held, with thirty or more bureaucrats to tell the world all of the good things they do to make life great for Indigenous peoples. My standing joke about this is that when I hear Canada testify in front of human rights bodies, I feel like jumping on the plane and going back home because it sounds like Canada has suddenly become such a paradise for Indigenous peoples. But of course, Canada works very hard to hide the actual facts from the prying eyes of the world.

That is why it is essential that Indigenous people attend these meetings to give their testimony of what are clearly Canadian abuses of their human and Indigenous rights.

The UN listens. The human rights committees also have their own researchers for every country and these researchers have a pretty clear idea of what is happening on the ground. That is why, at the end of each of these international hearings, you hear sharp rebukes to Canada about its treatment of Indigenous peoples and direct statements on the need for Canada to change its policies in order to comply with the human rights covenants and treaties it has signed.

It is important to know that when Canada is backed into a corner on Indigenous human rights issues, it is in fact forced to change its laws. We saw this with two landmark cases of sex discrimination against Indian women, where UN pressure forced Canada to make changes in laws toward Indigenous peoples.

One of these was the Lavell case, which was a challenge on human rights grounds of the Canadian law that stated that an Indian woman marrying a white man lost her status, while a white woman marrying an Indian man gained status. Jeannette Corbiere Lavell was an Anishinaabe woman from Wikwemikong and she grew up speaking Ojibwe and English. She was a woman of my generation who was ready to take on the world, and attended business college in North Bay before going on to work in Toronto as the executive secretary at the Native Canadian Centre of Toronto. She joined the Company of Young Canadians and travelled the country and, in 1965, she was even named that year's "Indian Princess of Canada." Along the way, she fell in love with David Lavell, a non-Native journalist, and they were married in 1970. Within weeks she received a letter that said her Indian status was terminated, that she was no longer deemed an Indian according to the Indian Act. She fought back all the way to the Supreme Court of Canada, which, as colonial courts are wont to do, upheld this obviously discriminatory law.

But it didn't end there. Indigenous women began to fight back with demonstrations and band council occupations against the outrageous law that deprived them and their children of their nationality and their heritage. Their fight culminated in the hundred-mile walk in 1979 from Oka, Quebec, to Ottawa to lay their objections in front of Parliament, and they went further with an international campaign that led to the discriminatory Canadian law being condemned by international human rights agencies.

The issue was put directly before the UN in 1982 when Sandra Lovelace, a Maliseet woman from the Tobique First Nation who had similarly lost her status under Canadian law, took her case to the UN Human Rights Committee. The committee found that, according to the International Covenant on Civil and Political Rights, the provision within Canada's *Indian Act* that stripped women of their status when marrying a non-Indian was invalid because it discriminated against Indian women. The Canadian government had no choice. Even though the legality of regulation had been confirmed by the Supreme Court of Canada, the government was forced to change it because of international obligations.

That is why the Canadian Parliament is not the final authority with Indigenous peoples and even the Supreme Court of Canada is not the final authority on Indigenous issues. When you go to law school, the law professors tell you the final authority in Canada is the Supreme Court of Canada. For most Canadians that is true, but for Indigenous peoples it is not. The higher authority is the international authority, because we are colonized nations and the international community has a duty to oversee decolonization around the world. And they have clearly stated in countless human rights documents that all nations have the right to self-determination, including Indigenous peoples.

These two principles, decolonization and the right to self-determination, are at the heart of our international struggle and it is in the international sphere that we will get the fairest hearing. And experience has shown that Canada, when pressed by the international community, will give ground.

CANADA'S LEGAL FIG LEAF

The fact that Canada plays the international game so intensely shows that they know that a lot is at stake. In trying to avoid the sweeping implications of Article 1 of the International human rights covenant that recognizes the rights of all "peoples" to self-determination, Canada really has only one card to play — and it is an exceedingly weak one. They try to jam all of the country's Indigenous peoples into Article 27 of the covenant. While Article 1 talks of Indigenous peoples as nations, Article 27 has been written as a protection for ethnic groups.

It states that:

> In those States in which ethnic, religious or
> linguistic minorities exist, persons belong-
> ing to such minorities shall not be denied the
> right, in community with the other members

> of their group, to enjoy their own culture, to
> profess and practise their own religion, or to
> use their own language.

What is completely absent here is the relationship Indigenous people have, by their very definition, to the land. Under Article 27, all that is required is that "minorities" are allowed to enjoy their language and culture undisturbed. So we are lumped in with ethnic Ukrainians in Winnipeg or Italians in Toronto or ethnic Germans in Kitchener as simply another part of the Canadian mosaic, which denies our existence as peoples and tries to duck responsibility for our inherent right to self-determination that they are honour-bound to respect as a signatory to the covenant. And of course, by turning us into ethnic minorities the path is open to steal our land, because the one right that no purely "ethnic" minority has is the right to the land.

But Canada has been called on this by the UN Human Rights Committee and it has so far ducked responsibility for replying. In international law "national minorities" and "Indigenous peoples" are two very different things and the patently dishonest attempt to conflate the two isn't fooling anyone except, unfortunately, the segments of the Canadian population who are ready to deny all rights to the Indigenous peoples within the country's borders.

CHAPTER 25
CERD: EARLY WARNING AND URGENT ACTION

The UN General Assembly and the Permanent Forum on Indigenous Issues are not the only international bodies where Indigenous peoples can get a hearing. In 2009, my Secwepemc people and the St'at'imc people in the British Columbian Interior took our case against the Canadian government's extinguishment policy to the Committee for the Elimination of Racial Discrimination (CERD) in Geneva.

We told the international body that the St'at'imc and Secwepemc Nations had never surrendered or ceded our inherent ownership (title) of our territorial lands. Nevertheless, we have been forced to live on Indian reserves that equal approximately 0.2 per cent of our original territories. This has resulted in our living in extreme and systemic poverty.

We also informed CERD that the Supreme Court of Canada had consistently affirmed that Aboriginal title has survived Canada's claims of sovereignty. Canada and British Columbia, instead of increasing our land base, has pursued a policy to extinguish our Aboriginal title under the modified and non-assertion models. This process was described in the Early Warning and Urgent Action submitted to CERD in

March 2009 and in the substantive submission presented on April 4, 2016.

We asked CERD to:

> recommend to Canada that Indigenous peoples be recognized as entitled to an exclusive land base that would make them self-supporting and that they have underlying title to their entire territory based on self-determination.

The Canadian representatives went before that committee to argue that the committee had no jurisdiction over Canada. The committee disagreed. They said they did have jurisdiction over Canada in this area because "Encroachment on the traditional lands of Indigenous peoples or forced removal of these peoples from their lands, in particular for the purpose of exploitation of natural resources" is a mandated concern of the committee, and this was clearly a case of the "encroachment of the traditional lands of Indigenous peoples."

In their response to Canada, the committee stated in a subsequent letter that final land claims agreements in a number of B.C. communities had been subject to processes that did not meet standards for fairness. This was a major rebuke to Canada, and above all to the whole B.C. treaty commission approach, which was the subject of our complaint.

In response, CERD called for the monitoring of future votes with independent mediators. They also questioned the negotiation of loan funding, and said it should not be used as a way to pressure Native people. And finally, they expressed concern over the incarceration of Aboriginal activists. With regards to Indigenous peoples, the world understands that at a fundamental level, Canada is a human rights abuser.

This was re-enforced during my most recent appearance before CERD. I went to Geneva to protest negotiations between four northern Secwepemc bands, of the seventeen bands in our nation, over the surrender of the north portion of our territory.

In our brief, we explained that land surrender negotiations were being held between the government and four Indian Act band chiefs who did not have the right to surrender Secwepemc land, because it is the whole Secwepemc people who are the title holders and not a handful of communities led by Indian Act chiefs.

When a vote on continuing the treaty negotiations took place, grassroots Secwepemc activists arrived to vote on the future of their territory but they were prevented by the RCMP from even entering the hall where the vote was to take place.

We brought our brief to the CERD meeting in Geneva and again the committee members listened. On October 3, 2016, the CERD chair wrote to the Canadian representative requesting that, before any further negotiations were undertaken, Canada provide information on steps it had taken to seek good faith agreements with Secwepemc peoples with regard to their lands and resources claims as well as:

> (a) Efforts made to ensure that representatives
> of all Secwepemc bands . . . are involved or
> at least are consulted about negotiations that
> may affect the collective land rights and terri-
> tory of the Secwepemc Nation.

And even more significant considering the Trudeau government's attempt to climb down on its UNDRIP commitments:

> (b) Measures to implement in good faith the right to free, prior and informed consent of the Secwepemc Nation and the St'at'imc Nation.

Until Canada satisfies these two basic requests, the government is in defiance of the UN anti-racism committee. This becomes another crack in Canada's facade into which we can insert our wedge and begin to hammer away. In July 2017, the 150th anniversary of Canadian Confederation, Canada will be facing the committee's questions about their actions on our territory in Geneva and our people will be there, once again, to give our testimony and to protest Canada's abuse of our rights.

The real problem today in British Columbia is that the government is not even putting forward a serious proposal. They know that most Indigenous groups will never accept what they are offering, but at the same time they know that if Indigenous people protest, they can simply get an injunction and then an enforcement order and then they can use armed force to push Indigenous peoples to the side while they carry on with their development without an agreement.

That works domestically, but when the United Nations sees that kind of activity, it is not accepted. The United Nations does not want to see armed force used. And just because you get an injunction order, it doesn't mean that you have legitimate right to the property that you are using armed force to acquire. That was very clear in Ipperwash,

Ontario, where the premier was quoted as saying, "I don't want to see those fucking Indians in that park" and the police took that to mean they had the right to go in with guns blazing — which they did, and they ended up killing Dudley George, an unarmed Indigenous man.

In the subsequent public enquiry, Justice Linden pointed out that when you have two legitimate interests making claim to an area, it is a principle of fundamental justice that one side should not be able to use armed force to eject the other. There has to be some kind of process toward a settlement. And that is the same position the United Nations takes. When there is lack of agreement, you cannot get away with simply resorting to force. And just because something is legal domestically, does not mean it conforms to international law. Indeed, in the majority of cases of international criminality and in all manner of war crimes, the defendant's actions were in complete compliance with domestic laws. Human rights experts in Geneva have seen it all, and they are not fooled.

CHAPTER 26

INTERNATIONAL RECOGNITION OF OUR PROPRIETARY RIGHTS

Fighting for Indigenous rights, including our land rights, at the human rights agencies must be a priority for all of our nations. But it goes even further than that. We are involved not only in a human rights struggle but an economic one. They stole our land for a reason — for the incredible, almost incalculable wealth it generates — and fighting for our economic rights puts us up against some of the most powerful forces on the planet. But strangely, it also gives us new opportunities to fight on the domestic front, because we can actually find allies there.

This means that we must not only continue to bring human rights violations to world bodies in search of international remedies, but we also have to bring attention to violations of our economic rights. The struggle of my community and the Indigenous Network on Economies and Trade provide an example of how our human rights fight is intimately linked to our fight for economic justice. A battle that began in our forests took us all the way to the US Department of Finance in Washington and the World Trade Organization in Geneva.

In 1999, when I was Neskonlith band chief, chairman of the Shuswap Nation Tribal Council and spokesperson for the Interior Alliance, our community joined Grand Chief Ronald Derrickson's Westbank First Nation by going out on our land to log with an Indigenous instead of a provincial permit. The government almost immediately took us to court in a case that is still active, with the Crown continuing to do everything that it can to delay the process because it fears that we will win — which I am sure we will if we can ever get it before a judge.

In the public relations battle with the government, we threatened to organize an international boycott of all B.C. forest products and this led us into talks with US environmental groups at a time when the whole Canada-US softwood lumber dispute was reaching its peak. We decided that the best way to bring Canada to the table was to intervene on the side of the US. In 2000, the Indigenous Network on Economies and Trade (INET) made submissions to the United States Department of Commerce arguing that Canada's policy of not recognizing Aboriginal and treaty rights in Canada was, in fact, an international trade subsidy to the Canadian forest industry. They were being freed from paying Indigenous peoples for our proprietary interest in the lumber — which had been recognized by the Supreme Court of Canada in the Delgamuukw decision. Our brief and its main principles were accepted by the Americans and by the NAFTA panel, despite fierce opposition by Canada.

When Canada appealed to the World Trade Organization in Geneva, Switzerland, we wrote a similar argument for them and they accepted it, which means that, even though Canada did not recognize Aboriginal title in the Secwepemc territory, when Canadian forest companies harvested those trees and sold them in Los Angeles there was still a proprietary interest by Indigenous peoples that has never been paid.

What NAFTA and the WTO are saying is that Canada and the forest companies were cheating the first owners of those trees (some of which were even older than Canada itself!) and because Canada was not paying them a fair share — or any share — it was able to sell the trees in the United States for below market value. Not paying Indigenous peoples for their ownership interest was therefore a trade subsidy to the Canadian industry.

During the last softwood lumber dispute, I spent many weeks lobbying in Washington, DC. I remember being told point blank that I was lobbying in the wrong capital. I should be in Ottawa. It was not until after the WTO and NAFTA made their decisions that Canada's refusal to recognize our Aboriginal and treaty rights is a trade subsidy that others came around to see that Washington, as well as New York and Geneva, could often move our struggle further than Ottawa was willing to do.

The softwood lumber issue is about to come around once more.

Canada and the United States prevented countervailing duties being applied to Canadian softwood lumber under a politically negotiated Softwood Lumber Agreement (SLA). The present SLA was entered into in 2006 and terminated in October 2016, without a new agreement in place.

Today, British Columbia still exports billions of dollars' worth of lumber, mainly in the form of 2x4s to the United States, and the small mill owners in the US are once again saying that Canadian timber sells less than what they can sell their timber for because Canada charges "less than market stumpage" for the trees. The American small mill owners again accuse Canada of subsidizing the Canadian forest interest by charging less than free market stumpage rates, and the remedy for this is to impose a countervailing duty on Canadian lumber exported to the US. So the old issues, it seems, remain and could be made worse for Canada with the arrival of an aggressive trader like Donald Trump in the White House. This means that we will once again be engaged in another Canada-US softwood lumber dispute.

We need to learn to defend our proprietary rights or we will continue to be shortchanged by Canada and the forestry industry. This time, with the Tsilhqot'in decision, our case is even stronger and we should once again launch a boycott of Canadian forest products until Aboriginal and treaty rights are taken into account regarding our access and benefits to a share of the $2.5 billion dollars' worth of our lumber being exported to the United States. We should begin meeting with Home Depot and other major buyers of B.C. softwood lumber and advise of the WTO and NAFTA decisions, and ask them to stop buying our timber from B.C. without our consent. We could advise them that we could take legal action against them if they continue to buy stolen lumber from Canada.

INET and the Interior Alliance should once again become involved in the upcoming Canada-US softwood lumber dispute to use our proprietary rights to reduce and eliminate the poverty the present system enforces our people to suffer under. Canada was furious with INET and the Interior Alliance when the WTO and NAFTA accepted our submissions, because they like having 100 per cent control over the wealth created by our trees. Indigenous peoples from north of the Medicine Line need to partner with our tribes south of the Medicine Line to fight for a mutual benefit from the harvesting of trees from our territory. We should fight for decision-making on "access and benefits" to our trees, and stop subsidizing the big timber companies that presently plunder our lands. Like all nations, we need to find a place for ourselves in the international marketplace.

This has already begun. For what it is worth, we have an AFN resolution supporting the Interior Alliance and INET's ongoing work on the Canada-US softwood lumber dispute. INET has established contact with Yakima Forest Products to arrange for a meeting with the Interior Alliance on the Canada-US dispute. The last softwood lumber dispute hurt a lot of the tribal softwood lumber mill owners in the US and it is through jointly lobbying with them for recognition of our proprietary rights in Washington, DC, that we will be able to put outside pressure on Canada to recognize our ownership of our trees.

Canada has already been on the offensive to try to block our impact. I was recently informed that the Canadian softwood lumber negotiating team from Global Affairs Canada (formerly External Affairs) had a conference call with some Indigenous leaders from B.C. As a result of that call, Grand Chief Ed John, who was one of the founders of the disastrous B.C. treaty process, drafted a resolution instructing the AFN to join Canada's softwood lumber negotiating team, which was an obvious ploy to weaken our international opposition to Canada's forestry policy. Thanks to behind-the-scenes efforts of people like Neskonlith chief Judy Wilson, Ed John's "Canadian compromise" was removed from the AFN resolution and the Interior Alliance resolution was passed.

It was the result of our effectiveness ten years ago that caused Global Affairs Canada to try to undermine us by bringing "compliant Indians" onto their negotiating team.

It is also why the province has been working on resource revenue sharing with Indigenous bands, so it can say that Indigenous peoples are getting paid for their Aboriginal and treaty rights. The real problem with that argument is that the formulas used are not hinged on our Aboriginal rights, but on a formula that is based on the province having full jurisdiction over our trees. These problems have to be brought up with our American tribes and the US government when we lobby in Washington, DC.

It does us no good to insist to each other in our own band halls that we own our trees. We need to say that in Washington, DC, and in Geneva, Switzerland. The future of our grandchildren depends on our courage and our thoughtfulness.

Clearly NAFTA and the WTO have already recognized that our Aboriginal title and right were not just a domestic issue that Canada can ignore or isolate with legal stumbling blocks. Our Aboriginal title and rights are recognized at the international financial level as a real proprietary interest, just as our Indigenous right to self-determination is recognized at the UN and in international human rights bodies.

The challenge, of course, is to force the Canadian government and the people of Canada to live up to international standards in its treatment of Indigenous peoples within its borders. And the point of the spear is our insistence that the Trudeau government be held to its own promise to implement the UN Declaration of Rights of Indigenous Peoples. That is where we can make our greatest breakthrough.

CHAPTER 27

UNDRIP AND THE TRUDEAU BETRAYAL

So now we arrive squarely back at UNDRIP. All of our rights that were recognized under Article 1 of the United Nations covenant are reaffirmed and expanded in the UN Declaration of the Rights of Indigenous Peoples.

The fact that the Trudeau government is trying to diminish these fundamental rights that were awarded to all Indigenous peoples in 2007 by an overwhelming vote of the General Assembly is very close to unforgivable. But it is also part of a long history of Canadian treachery on the world stage when it comes to Indigenous peoples.

Fighting against human rights for Indigenous peoples internationally has been a staple of Canadian governments since Iroquois leader Deskaheh visited the League of Nations in 1923–24 to ask for standing for his people. He very nearly had the world body accept Iroquois membership until the British delegation, acting for Canada, swooped in to block it. Canada tried the same thing when UNDRIP was being negotiated in the 2000s. Working in conjunction with the other major settler states — the US, Australia and New Zealand — they tried desperately to block the passage of UNDRIP by the UN General Assembly.

UNDRIP
Self - determination

Article 3

Indigenous peoples have the right of self-determination. By virtue of that right they freely determine their political status and freely pursue their economic, social and cultural development.

16-04-29

But this time they failed in a spectacular fashion. Included on page 195 is the voting card that was put out by the UN the moment the vote was taken in September 2007.

There were 143 yes votes in favour of UNDRIP, 4 no votes and 11 abstentions. When that vote was about to be taken, I was very worried that we would lose. Indigenous peoples had been lobbying for over twenty years on this and a lot of countries, not just the four who were actively campaigning against it, were not very enthusiastic about it. Countries like China and many of the African nations didn't want to support it because of ongoing issues they had with Indigenous peoples in their own countries. In Africa many of the tribal groups were demanding to return to their self-governing tribal territories — which often spread across two or more of the colonial states. So many of the African nations were reluctant to support UNDRIP because they were concerned it would reawaken the issue of independent tribal territories and state boundaries. But, finally, the case for Indigenous rights in the world was too compelling. When it went to a vote, the only countries that opposed it were the Anglo-settler states of Canada, the United States, Australia and New Zealand.

Why Canada opposed it was clear from a simple glance at the contents. UNDRIP guarantees Indigenous peoples the right to our nationality, which the government does everything it can to undermine. It further recognizes our "right to belong to an indigenous community or nation, in accordance with the traditions and customs of the community or nation concerned."

UNDRIP calls for the cessation of violence against us, "including forcibly removing children of the group to another group." It demands our protection from "any action which has the aim or effect of dispossessing us of our lands, territories or resources." It says states must provide restitution "with respect to their cultural, intellectual, religious and spiritual property taken without their free, prior and informed consent or in violation of their laws, traditions and customs."

UNDRIP clearly states that "Indigenous peoples have the right to establish and control their educational systems and institutions providing education in their own languages." It declares: "States shall consult and cooperate in good faith with the indigenous peoples concerned through their own representative institutions in order to obtain their free, prior and informed consent before adopting and implementing legislative or administrative measures that may affect them."

UNDRIP demands that states "take measures, in conjunction with indigenous peoples, to ensure that indigenous women and children enjoy the full protection and guarantees against all forms of violence and discrimination."

Most important of all, UNDRIP is unequivocal on the land question: "Indigenous peoples have the right to the lands, territories and resources which they have traditionally owned, occupied or otherwise used or acquired" and "Indigenous peoples have the right to own, use, develop and control the lands, territories and resources that they possess by reason of traditional ownership or other traditional occupation or use." It also states that "Indigenous peoples have the right to the conservation and protection of the environment and the productive capacity of their lands or territories and resources."

To give weight to all of these fundamental rights, UNDRIP is unambiguous on our right to self-determination, which is denied in a thousand ways by the Canadian government, in every syllable of the racist *Indian Act* that still is used to control our lives. In Article 3, UNDRIP states:

> Indigenous peoples have the right to self-determination. By virtue of that right they freely determine their political status and freely pursue their economic, social and cultural development.

What UNDRIP does not threaten is the sovereignty of Canada. The final article in the declaration addresses the issue of territorial integrity. Canada falsely claims that the right to self-determination could lead to secession, that Indigenous peoples would pull out of Canada in the way Quebec has threatened to pull out. This was touched on earlier but it bears a fuller discussion here.

United Nations Declaration on Rights of Indigenous peoples

UNITED NATIONS
GENERAL ASSEMBLY
PLENARY MEETING: 107
RECORDED VOTE ADOPTED

DATE: 13 SEP 07
TIME: 12:29 PM
VOTE: 1

YES: 143
NO: 4
ABSTAIN: 11

Abstain: Azerbaijan Bangladesh Bhutan Burundi Colombia Georgia Kenya Nigeria Russian Federation Samoa Ukraine.

Y Afghanista Y Albania
Y Algeria
Y Andorra
Y Angola
Y Antigua and Barbuda
Y Argentina
Y Armenia
N Australia
Y Austria
Y Bahamas
Y Bahrain
Y Barbados
Y Belarus
Y Belgium
Y Belize
Y Benin
Y Bolivia
Y Bosnia/Herzegovina
Y Botswana
Y Brazil
Y Brunei Dar-salam
Y Bulgaria
Y Burkina Faso
Y Cambodia
Y Cameroon
N Canada
Y Cape Verde
Y Central Afr Rep
Y Chile
Y China
Y Comoros
Y Congo
Y Costa Rica
Y Croatia
Y Cuba
Y Cyprus
Y Czech Republic
Y Democratic People's Republic of Korea
Y Democratic Republic of the Congo
Y Denmark
Y Djibouti
Y Dominica
Y Dominican Republic
Y Ecuador
Y Egypt
Y El Salvador
Y Estonia
Y Finland
Y FrAnce

Y Gabon
Y Germany
Y Ghana
Y Greece
Y Guatemala
Y Guinea
Y Guyana
Y Haiti
Y Honduras
Y Hungary
Y Iceland
Y India
Y Indonesia
Y Iran
Y Iraq
Y Ireland
Y Italy
Y Jamaica
Y Japan
Y Jordan
Y Kazakhstan
Y Kuwait
Y Lao People's Democratic Republic
Y Latvia
Y Lebanon
Y Lesotho
Y Liberia
Y Libya
Y Liechtenstein
Y Lithuania
Y Luxembourg
Y Madagascar
Y Malawi
Y Malaysia
Y Maldives
Y Mali
Y Malta
Y Mauritius
Y Mexico
Y Micronesia (Federated States of)
Y Moldova
Y Monaco
Y Mongolia
Y Mozambique
Y Myanmar
Y Namibia
Y Nepal
Y Netherlands
N New Zealand

Y Nicaragua
Y Niger
Y Norway
Y Oman
Y Pakistan
Y Panama
Y Paraguay
Y Peru
Y Philippines
Y Poland
Y Portugal
Y Qatar
Y Republic of Korea
Y Saint Lucia
Y Saint Vincent and the Grenadines
Y San Marino
Y Saudi Arabia
Y Senegal
Y Serbia
Y Sierra Leone
Y Singapore
Y Slovakia
Y Slovenia
Y South Africa
Y Spain
Y Sri Lanka
Y Sudan
Y Suriname
Y Swaziland
Y Sweden
Y Switzerland
Y Syria
Y Thailand
Y The former Yugoslav Republic of Macedonia
Y Timor-Leste
Y Trinidad and Tobago
Y Tunisia Turkey
Y United Arab Emirates
Y United Kingdom
Y United Republic of Tanzania
N United States
Y Uruguay
Y Venezuela
Y Viet Nam
Y Yemen
Y Zambia
Y Zimbabwe

Only four countries voted against the UN Declaration on Rights of Indigenous Peoples: Canada and the three other Anglo settler states, the US, Australia and New Zealand.

From the founding of the Parti Québécois in 1968 into the 2000s, the federal government was fairly obsessed with the issue of Quebec separation. After the near-miss referendum in 1995, the federal government sought for a legal way to get a grip on the issue with a reference on what, exactly, were the rights of provinces to secede from Confederation. To find out, Chrétien sent the issue to the Supreme Court for a reference, with the federal government arguing for the curtailing of the rights of Quebec to secede. The court finally ruled that Quebec did, indeed, have the right to hold a referendum on the issue, but that it could not declare independence unilaterally because they were not oppressed. They would have to negotiate the terms of secession with Canada.

The irony here, of course, it that Native people are oppressed. You only have to apply international criteria, or even the international well-being index that puts Canada close to number one and Indigenous peoples within its borders down near number eighty. So in fact, Indigenous nations could make a convincing case even to the Supreme Court of Canada about our right to secede from Canada. But this has never been our goal. Indigenous peoples are not trying to dismember Canada. Indigenous peoples want recognition of our Aboriginal and treaty rights on the ground, we want our proprietary interest in the land recognized and our right to self-determination respected. All of this can be done within the Canadian space. In fact, what we are really saying — what we have been saying all along — is that Aboriginal title is really the foundation of Canada and Canadian territorial integrity.

The right that UNDRIP confers on our peoples is a declaration of independence of our nations within the Canadian space, and that is the standard that the world is holding Canada to. This is the standard that we must hold Canada to and what Canada seemed to finally have accepted on May 10, 2016, when Justin Trudeau's Indigenous and Northern Affairs Minister Carolyn Bennett went to New York to pledge to fully implement the UN Declaration on the Rights of Indigenous Peoples.

Clearly, she was indicating a major change of course. In 2007, immediately after the UN General Assembly had overwhelmingly voted to endorse it, Canadian UN ambassador John McNee explained Canada's no vote by claiming that Canada had long protected and promoted Indigenous peoples' rights at home, "in a way that was consistent with its Constitution and treaties," and also abroad, where its development programs aimed at improving Indigenous peoples' lives. McNee said Canada had played an active role in the Geneva process and had proposed a text that could "promote Indigenous peoples' fundamental freedoms while fostering harmony between Indigenous peoples and states." (Note he spoke about Indigenous peoples' "freedoms" but not our rights.) He claimed that UNDRIP was vague, then went on to list the specifics, particularly the right to self-determination and the right to free prior informed consent as "especially problematic." McNee insisted that "rights of Indigenous peoples had to be 'better balanced.'" Finally, McNee said, Canada considered UNDRIP to be "non-binding, and without domestic effect."

When he was campaigning for office, Justin Trudeau said he would be reversing all that. UNDRIP would be fully implemented and binding in Canada. That was why there was that flash of euphoria among our peoples at the announcement. And the devastating disappointment when we were told by Jody Wilson-Raybould, a former regional chief of the Assembly of First Nations and now the Minister of Justice in the Trudeau cabinet, that UNDRIP really was unworkable as it is and what they had really adopted was some kind of mysterious "Canadian version." In a flash, Canada had returned to its 2006 contra position of accepting UNDRIP to be once again "non-binding, and without domestic effect."

This is Canada's greatest betrayal of this century, and it was made less than a year after Trudeau took office with a promise to fully adopt UNDRIP into Canadian law.

We must not let this betrayal stand. We must insist international law be respected in Canada and no one, not the prime minister or the Minister of Indigenous and Northern Affairs, or a Liberal minister with a status card, can tell us that all forty-six articles of the UN Declaration of the Rights of Indigenous Peoples, exactly as written, do not apply to Indigenous peoples living within the Canadian space. That declaration does not belong to Justin Trudeau, or Indigenous and Northern Affairs Minister Bennett or Justice Minister Jody Wilson-Raybould. It belongs to us, the 370 million Indigenous peoples of the world. And we will demand it is respected in every article, every clause, every word. This, finally, is our Charter of Rights and Freedoms, and settler societies must understand we will not, we cannot, accept anything less.

PART 6
FALSE RECONCILIATION

CHAPTER 28

THE RECONCILIATION SWAT TEAM

In *Unsettling Canada*, I wrote about the SWAT team, for "Special Words And Tactics," that my colleague Russell Diabo says operates inside the Department of Indigenous and Northern Affairs. It is this group, he says, that originally called the collection of delegated municipal-style powers that are offered to Indigenous people "self-government." The SWAT team was also there to describe the extinguishment of our Aboriginal title and rights as a much nicer sounding "surrender and grant back" process, and then, when that was also condemned by the international community, they described it as "modifying" our rights and title.

It appears that the SWAT team is now having a field day with "reconciliation." The term "reconciliation" now covers any and all manipulations or diminution of our rights and title. The government and the Canadian people have fallen in love with reconciliation. They do not really seem to understand the concept but they truly love that word. Everything is reconciliation. When they join a round dance, they call that reconciliation. When their eyes tear up in discussing our poverty, that is reconciliation. At the same time, when they are denying our constitutional rights, they call that reconciliation of Aboriginal title with Crown title. In fact, every new plan to steal from us is called reconciliation. Among these are the Reconciliation Framework Agreements. Dr. Taiaiake Alfred probably said it best when he characterized "reconciliation as recolonization." That is what it has become in the hands of the Trudeau government, and sadly, they are finding allies among our people.

To truly reconcile Aboriginal and Crown title, Canada and the provinces would first have to recognize and affirm our Aboriginal and treaty rights on the ground. Then we can negotiate an agreement on the details of implementation. Anything less is not to seek reconciliation, but surrender.

The federal and provincial governments in Canada, and a number of the high-profile Indigenous leaders who are directly or indirectly paid by these governments, speak incessantly about reconciliation without demanding recognition of our title and recompense for past abuses. Some of these paid Indigenous leaders use this longing for reconciliation as a way to express their love for their paymasters and, even though Canada has stolen their people's lands, they want to reconcile their hearts with Canadians. It is almost like they want the whites to forgive them for being Indigenous, so they can all move on together and celebrate July 1 as the birth of their nation and forget about the past. Many Canadians are obviously delighted by this sort of meaningless, no-strings-attached "reconciliation." For them, it is having your cake and eating it too. You not only get to keep the stolen land, you are forgiven for the theft and you can emotionally reconcile all this with our leaders (who you have, in fact, hired for that purpose).

In the interest of spreading confusion — which is always in their interest — the government is also using the term "reconciliation" in the legal sense of reconciling Aboriginal and Crown title. But in this use of "reconciliation" they really mean extinguishment of our title and rights.

My father was one of the first Indigenous leaders calling for Indian self-government, but after the Department of Indian Affairs defined what they meant — basically giving us municipal powers — he campaigned vigorously against the government's self-government fraud. That warped policy is still being imposed now and the government's "reconciliation" of Crown and Aboriginal title is as phoney as their self-government proposals.

But for those of us in struggle for our land and our people's survival, this one-sided reconciliation is not only distasteful, it is extraordinarily harmful. In embracing this form of reconciliation, our neocolonial leadership gives the world the image that we do not, after all, need self-determination because the colonial system where all our land remains under federal and provincial control is working. Official Indigenous leadership cooperation in this regard is all the proof they need. They are giving the world the image that Canada stole our land fair and square and is welcome to keep it.

In fact, you can only get rid of the colonial privilege of Canada and the provinces making 100 per cent of decisions over our land by creating tension and economic uncertainty both domestically and internationally. Our colonial masters will not give up their privilege without intense pressure from below. They will not do it out of respect. Colonialists, by definition, do not respect the Indigenous peoples they are dominating. We are a reminder to them of their land theft, their original sin, and they want us hidden away or absorbed through assimilation. This is not a hidden agenda, it was openly proclaimed as Canadian policy for most of the first hundred years of the country's life. Then, when the racism of this statement became obvious, they stopped saying this out loud. But they continued with policies designed to carry it out.

All that talk about respect and reconciliation is self-serving rhetoric, because if the prime minister and the premiers actually respected Indigenous peoples, they would recognize that they must first respect and affirm our Indigenous rights to our lands before real reconciliation is even logically possible.

CHAPTER 29
RECONCILIATION FRAMEWORK AGREEMENTS

The overriding objective in all of the government's dealing with Indigenous peoples is to have continued unfettered access and control over Indigenous lands. Today, they have armies of civil servants working on new schemes to get us to surrender our title and rights and whatever they come up with, they are certain to call it "reconciliation." Thus the "Reconciliation Framework Agreements" were born.

Even though I know this is dry material for some — and I do not blame you if you decide to skip ahead to the next chapter — I feel we have to look closely at these Reconciliation Framework Agreements (RFA) to see how devious governments are in their handling of our rights. And how we must always stay clear in our own minds about what we are after.

These agreements grew out of the inconsistency between the government's business-as-usual political strategy and the effect of the court decisions recognizing our Aboriginal title, which has tossed a large measure of economic uncertainty into the mix. The uncertainty is increased because negotiations under the comprehensive land claims policy used in the B.C. treaty process have largely been unsuccessful. This has meant that industry is putting pressure on governments to enter into separate agreements with Indigenous peoples on an industry-by-industry basis so they can get access to the resources on Aboriginal title lands without waiting for treaties to be signed.

To fulfill its legal responsibility for consultation and accommodation, the provincial government has been vigorously pursuing these reconciliation agreements with Indigenous peoples who are not negotiating under the comprehensive land claims policy. The real problem with the reconciliation agreements is that they relieve pressure on the provincial government and free up our lands for industry, but do not provide any real benefit to Indigenous peoples.

With the land claims talks going nowhere, industry knows we can challenge the government's jurisdiction and claim ownership over our lands and resources. Hence, the province needs to get our approval to sell off our natural wealth under provincial jurisdiction. Controlling access and benefits to the natural wealth of our territories is how the B.C. government exists and how the settler economy becomes rich. The ultimate purpose of the RFA is to make Aboriginal rights subject to provincial jurisdiction, and Aboriginal rights under these RFAs are basically plugged into existing provincial government processes and activities. The province takes the lead role in these discussions simply because their very purpose serves their economic and political interests, while at the same time they falsely claim to have disposed of the provincial government's obligation to "consult" with Indigenous peoples.

In the purpose section of the RFA, the province clearly establishes that it wants and needs economic certainty for the B.C. economy to use our lands (Aboriginal title) and resources (Aboriginal rights) for their exclusive benefit:

> 2.1 The Parties acknowledge that the shared decision making structures and processes described in this Agreement are *intended to mitigate, reduce or avoid disputes over land and resources management* and are intended in part to reduce the need for the Parties to use formal dispute resolution mechanisms.

What does the RFA offer Indigenous peoples for giving the provincial government economic certainty? Indigenous peoples only get vague and limited benefits, such as being in an "engagement process" with the province, and we are promised "economic and resource revenue sharing opportunities in accordance with prevailing provincial policy and mandates."

There are absolutely no economic guarantees or securities for Indigenous peoples or undertakings to reduce and eliminate the poverty we experience.

The province has become used to having 100 per cent power to issue hunting and fishing permits, forestry licences, grazing permits, mining permits, water licences, grant fee simple on Crown land and make rules over parks and the limited environmental protection regulations that remain. But because Aboriginal title and rights have been recognized on the ground by the Supreme Court of Canada they are searching for a mechanism to void our rights. This is made explicit in the RFA, which calls upon the elected Indigenous leaders to concede that this agreement will be ruled under federal and provincial law. It is stated quite clearly: "This

Agreement is to be governed by the applicable laws of Canada and British Columbia."

This is in total contradiction, for example, of the legal case the Secwepemc people are bringing forward claiming jurisdiction over forestry based on our Aboriginal title and rights and on our Indigenous laws. This is imperative because our laws are based on our land and we cannot claim our land through or under federal and provincial government laws.

I look at these agreements, and what they do is give the province "certainty" in exploiting our land but they only offer us the power to "engage" in that process but nothing else. In fact, it will probably cost us more money than they are willing to fund to be part of this process. The few hundreds of thousands of dollars that the province throws out in the agreement would be a mere fraction of what it would cost to do the work that needs to be done in researching our rights and environmental impacts. Furthermore, it would be an insignificant fraction of what would be taken out of our land. In many ways, these reconciliation agreements are modern-day versions of the beads and trinkets deals the first Europeans offered us. They are insulting.

The Secwepemc Reconciliation Framework Agreement tries to say it will not affect Secwepemc Aboriginal title and rights, but it clearly will. The reconciliation process will fulfill the duty of the province to consult with Indigenous peoples and the non-Secwepemc projects will thus become a legitimate third party interest in our Aboriginal title and territory. Our people may get a few dollars under the revenues sharing agreement, but this process is not based on our Aboriginal title and rights and instead fits more logically into the "bribes" category. In the end, it will probably be considered own source revenue and be deducted from federal money and we will be left with nothing at all.

In regards to mines, this would mean that the people living during the life of the mine will get a small amount of cash for the community when the mine is in operation, but future generations will get no money and only be left with the pollution of the tailings. Similarly, the government really has no formula for pipelines and their ongoing and potentially disastrous impact on our lands. The Secwepemc Reconciliation Framework Agreement is really a way to circumvent our Aboriginal title and rights, leaving future generations to deal with the consequences of these third party interests in our territory.

It is far wiser to refuse to accept any of these limited agreements within the narrow process in which they are offered. The existing uncertainty is, in fact, the biggest power we have for pushing the federal government to change the present extinguishment policy. We should use this power to get recognition and affirmation of our Aboriginal title and rights for all future generations. We should not be cashing in for a few dollars of short-term gain.

Our objective is to build our self-government based on our right to self-determination and build an Indigenous economy, and not to be tacked on as an afterthought to the federal and provincial economies. We need to stand up for more than just jobs, business opportunities and limited revenue sharing agreements. We need to build an Indigenous economy based on recognition and affirmation of our Aboriginal title and rights and for sustainable development on our lands.

We know from experience that the B.C. economy has impoverished our peoples systematically for generation after generation, ever since B.C. was set up as an apartheid colony in 1858. We know from experience that the existing federal and provincial economies are based on not recognizing our Aboriginal title and rights. Once again — in B.C. all Indian reserves make up 0.36 per cent of all B.C. lands. This means that the B.C. government is in charge of 99.64 per cent of our territory in what is now private and "Crown land." This is why we are poor.

We cannot trust the B.C. government and when you sit down to negotiate these arrangements with a government that refuses, up front, to deal with Aboriginal title and rights you are undermining the economic power we have in exchange for what amounts to pocket change that will largely be spent on the process itself. What little we get in these deals goes to our consultants and virtually nothing makes it to our far too numerous poor people or to sustainable economic investments for our future. There is certainly no money in these deals to give to our grandchildren, whose rights are being impacted. I believe that if we cannot see money and benefits accrue to our grandkids we should not accept any agreement that compromises our land by third party provincial government economic interests.

The reason the province is pushing these agreements is clearly to sidestep dealing with the substantive issues of recognition and affirmation of Aboriginal title and rights and to be able to carry on with business-as-usual in the face of the economic uncertainty caused by the fact that Indigenous peoples do have proprietary and economic rights in their traditional territory. This reconciliation process merely supports the B.C. economy. It does nothing to build up our Indigenous economy. It is another of the happy-faced reconciliation frauds being imposed on our people.

PART 7
STANDING OUR GROUND

CHAPTER 30
DEFENDING OUR LAND

Indigenous peoples from around the world suffer dispropor-
tionately, often exponentially, higher rates of poverty,
health problems, sky-high incarceration rates, suicides and
severely reduced life expectancies. We all know this. The
list is depressingly familiar, but what lies behind it is also a
small miracle. We are still here. We are still fighting. And
we know the list outlines only the symptoms of our oppression. The cure is what we always have been and always will
be fighting for: to get the colonial authorities to respect our
Creator-given rights to our land and our inalienable right —
as members of the family of nations — to self-determination.

To address the causes of our oppression, Indigenous
peoples need to seek fundamental change in the way our
worlds are structured. And to push forward with that
change, we need to create the kind of political tension
that eradicated segregation in the United States and the
type of international coalition that helped end apartheid
in South Africa. In Canada, the primary force behind
the status quo is colonialism. Colonialism is the system
Europeans used to dominate the world. With regards to
Indigenous peoples, colonialism is shaped by dispossession,

dependency, economic exploitation and oppression. These forces are deeply integrated into the constitutional and legal systems of countries like Canada and they have to be challenged at every turn.

The Defenders of the Land and Idle No More are part of the Indigenous movements that are calling upon Indigenous peoples to fundamentally challenge the status quo. They are in practical terms raising the issues of dispossession, dependency and economic exploitation. The real problem with doing this is that you will be confronted by the systemic power of the status quo wanting to maintain control over Indigenous peoples. I know this from the Sun Peaks dispute, where the head-smashing RCMP squads were sent in waves against my people, including against my own children, and more recent disputes like the battle to stop fracking at Elsipogtog where the same tactics were used. When they see you standing up, they will do everything to try to knock you down again. That is why we need Defenders.

The ongoing and relentless land conflicts — expressed in sit-ins, demonstrations, blockades and other ways of asserting ownership — from my father's generation to my own to those of my children and grandchildren, show that Indigenous peoples in Canada refuse to accept that the *Constitution Act*s of 1867 or 1982 gave a moral or, in the international sense, a legal right to Canada and its provinces to confiscate and destroy our land. The frequent use of paramilitary forces like the RCMP and at times the Canadian military to suppress our peoples and trample on our Aboriginal and treaty rights reflects the fact that we are not Canadian. The "persistent disparity," as the UN Special Rapporteur recently put it, between Indigenous peoples and the settlers reaffirms that we are not Canadians.

This is demonstrated most clearly in the UN international standard of living index that put Canada as number one and Indigenous peoples in Canada at seventy-eight, down with the impoverished third world countries.

That is why our sympathies and solidarity go out to all those on the front line struggling to reoccupy and reassert their sovereignty on their lands. Members of my own family and many of my dear friends have taken and continue to take this courageous stand.

I know there are also a few of my people who are part of the neocolonial structure. This is disheartening. But for the fighters, I hope the Creator gives them the courage to persist through the difficult times ahead. Canada and the provinces have only one objective when they engage in colonial oppression and that is colonial rule, which means they will try to crush your spirit and your independence. Be strong. You are on the right side in the moral sense. And if we build a strong and fearless people's resistance, you will also be on the right side of history.

CHAPTER 31
THE LEGAL BILLY CLUB

At the end of our acts of defiance, we are often met with the business end of the police truncheon. But the process of attacking us usually begins weeks and even months earlier, when the state takes in hand its legal billy club: the court injunction.

The weight of this club is provided by the racist colonial doctrines of discovery claiming that we have been fully and irreversibly dispossessed of our territories. That is the underpinning behind the Canadian state's vision of Crown land, and it is the force behind the injunctions that industry and governments use to get enforcement orders that allows them to use the police, paramilitaries and even the army to crush our efforts to inhabit the lands given to us by our Creator.

As soon as we leave our reserves to return to our land, government and industry take collateral colonial legal action in the form of the court injunction. By that means they instantly transform the Royal Canadian Mounted Police, the Ontario Provincial Police, the Sûreté du Quebec or whatever security force is on the scene into an attack force against us. If we continue to resist, they escalate to the Canadian military, and it is notable that regarding potential opposition to pipelines the Trudeau government has already specifically warned that it will use the Canadian military against any of its citizens who try to stand in the way of the full exploitation of the country's petroleum resources.

The injunction, enforcement orders, and prosecution for contempt of court are the means by which our assertion of our rights on the ground is instantly criminalized by the Canadian state, even when it is clear that we have a very good legal case to the land in question. Colonial courts do not take into account our legal rights when issuing injunctions — they operate purely on the status quo and such unlofty principles as the "balance of convenience." Injunctions are therefore the aces up the sleeve of the government and industry when land is being contested. They are generally quickly granted to government and industry but rarely to Indigenous peoples. Even when we have a clear-cut case for proprietorship over our land, injunctions are granted "on the balance of convenience" to government and industry and our further activity on the land is instantly criminalized.

Injunctions are an ideal tool of oppression because they allow government and industry to skirt the substantive legal issues behind Indigenous rights to follow only the status quo concept that our lands are, at present, in possession of the settler state and until we overturn this fact, we do not have the right to exercise our own jurisdiction there.

We saw the devastating effect of injunctions as a tool to criminalize our activities in my own community, Neskonlith. When I was chief, a group of our youth and Elders moved up the mountain and set up a camp at the foot of the new Sun Peaks ski resort development on our Aboriginal title lands.

At first, the federal government avoided getting involved in this dispute and let the province deal with it. The province and Sun Peaks, which was owned by Nippon Cable, a Japanese multi-national, took collateral legal action to avoid negotiating a mutually agreeable solution to this dispute. They resorted to injunctions and enforcement orders against our people, who were peacefully camping at the entrance to the construction site.

The end product of this process is often our men, women and Elders thrown face down onto the ground with handcuffs locked on their wrists. But it all begins in a surprisingly genteel manner. Polite and well-dressed and well-groomed corporate lawyers appear before a court to state that a group of Indigenous people — in our case at Sun Peaks it was a small group of youth and Elders — have moved onto and are inhabiting or blocking a section of their Aboriginal title land. They point out that the Crown does not acknowledge the Aboriginal title and even if the issue is before the courts, argues the balance of convenience for an injunction while cases are being decided elsewhere. In such cases, colonial courts generally side with the corporations and the injunctions are granted. Then the courtly manners are dispensed with. The Crown is free to show its teeth. They send in the police to move in and break heads and make arrests if we do not disperse on their command.

In our Sun Peaks dispute, over fifty arrests were made over several years and Indigenous people, including my own daughters, spent months in jail. This is unacceptable in our country. It is unacceptable anywhere in the world to have Indigenous people jailed simply for refusing to leave their own land. It is when we stand our ground we see that ultimately the power is based only on the violence they can bring to bear against us. We will fight violence with resistance and calls for justice within Canada and internationally.

As my friend Dr. Shiri Pasternak has written, "blockades are the meeting of settler and Indigenous legal orders — and not just as some tactic of civil disobedience." We must continue to assert our legal rights over our land, no matter what the consequences. And we will meet settler law at the blockade with our own Indigenous law and Aboriginal title and rights to the land.

What is most frustrating when the government uses the courts against us is the fact that, when the tables are turned and the courts actually support us, the government thinks nothing of ignoring them to the point of openly breaching court orders.

I have pointed to it before and it is one of the most worrying aspects of Canada's treatment toward Indigenous peoples: when our rights are at stake, the Canadian government consistently ignores rulings of its own courts. This should worry Canadians as well. When the judicial branch is no longer a check on executive power, democracy itself is at stake. But this is the situation in Canada with regards to Indigenous law.

For example, the federal government has maintained its comprehensive claims policy that employs a "modification" and "non-assertion" approach resulting in the de facto extinguishment of Aboriginal title, despite the fact that the federal government is required to act as a fiduciary to Indigenous peoples and to protect and implement Aboriginal title and rights, which are recognized and affirmed by Section 35 of the Canadian Constitution. As such, there is an affirmative obligation on the federal government to bring its laws and policies in line with the highest law in the country, the Canadian *Constitution Act*, and the highest court in the country, the Supreme Court of Canada.

The federal government has implemented Supreme Court of Canada decisions regarding other issues, such as same sex marriage and safe injection sites, but not regarding Aboriginal title and rights, although they have an even more stringent obligation in that regard as the fiduciary. The result is a constitutional breach, where the executive branch (the government) does not implement the binding rulings of the judiciary branch and the Constitution, the highest expression of the legislative branch. In turn, Indigenous peoples who assert and exercise their Aboriginal title and rights rather than negotiating under policies that violate the Constitution and international human rights standards are subject to executive action and criminalization.

The federal government continues to fail to live up to its constitutional obligations as a fiduciary, opposing judgements in favour of Indigenous rights instead of taking the side of Indigenous peoples. At the same time, the provincial governments do not hesitate to resort to violence against our people if we try to stand up for our rights.

CHAPTER 32
BLOCKADING A MINE

I never completed my law degree and was never called to the bar, but I do spend an inordinate amount of time in courts — although almost always sitting behind the defendants.

This time, the Crown is seeking an injunction against our people for blockading the Red Chris Mine. In our case, we set out the fundamental aspects of Aboriginal title and our constitutional rights. But we also have to explain to the court that our traditional food economy is still how our families compensate for being forced onto social assistance. We depend on our territory for our livelihood. Mining turns this economic system upside down, especially in light of the Imperial Metals catastrophic tailings spill that happened in Secwepemc territory near Likely, B.C., on August 4, 2014. Indigenous peoples do not trust federal and provincial mining and environmental laws and a disaster like the Mount Polley tailings pond spill raises serious questions about the Red Chris Mine, which is another Imperial Metals property. After Mount Polley, no Imperial Metals mine will have any credibility for our people.

The Red Chris Mine is a particular threat. It is to be built in the Sacred Headwaters region of the Stikine, Nass and Skeena rivers, three of B.C.'s most important salmon bearing rivers. This region is also the spawning ground for rainbow trout and home of mountain goats, grizzly bears, wolverines, stone sheep and caribou. Some have called it Canada's Serengeti. The planned tailings pond would be of the same design as the one that only a year earlier had dumped millions of litres of poisons in the local creeks, rivers and lakes.

Indigenous people had blockaded the site to prevent the Imperial Metals drillers from entering and when they were hauled into court, they told the judge that they did not agree that Crown title is the underlying title in their territory nor did they agree that Aboriginal title has been supplanted by Crown title.

Indigenous peoples fighting for their Aboriginal title and rights must fundamentally challenge the use of injunctions in regard to unresolved Aboriginal title and rights. The injunction should be viewed in terms of the colonial law versus the recognition and affirmation of Aboriginal title and rights. We believe governments must not use injunctions to bulldoze away our rights or as a cover for inadequate laws and policies toward Indigenous peoples and their legal and political rights.

The courts and the balance of convenience must not only weigh government control and industries' monetary interests, but also the cultural rights, the lives, the livelihood, and the constitutionally and, indeed, internationally recognized land and cultural rights of Indigenous peoples.

Unjust federal and provincial laws, policies and objectives require Indigenous peoples to personally defend our land, where we have very limited or no control over decisions made over our land. It is important for the business and investment community to understand that it is the responsibility of governments to work out these differences. That is why the British Columbia treaty process is a twenty-year failed process.

Canada really does not have any process to resolve the Red Chris dispute. Indigenous peoples do not take action simply to confront the Royal Canadian Mounted Police or because we like going to jail or seeing our children and our Elders carted off in handcuffs. We do not take our liberty and the liberty of our families so lightly. But we see very few alternatives in Canada today.

Lack of mutually agreed upon policies puts a lot of pressure on the rightful title holders who depend on their Aboriginal title and rights to put food on the table. The rightful title holders have a legal obligation and human right to defend not only their Aboriginal title and rights but the Aboriginal title and rights of future generations, especially in view of mining operations where the damage can last for many generations. Indigenous peoples are carrying on traditional activities on these lands right now and it is these activities that give content to Indigenous laws and establish our own jurisdiction over our Aboriginal title lands.

While I was listening to the Imperial Metals lawyers drone on about how we had no rights, I must admit I was thinking of the phoney smiles and hugs we were receiving from Prime Minister Trudeau. If there had been "real change" in Canada's policy toward Indigenous peoples you would see it first here, on the front lines. But the justice department, now headed by an Indigenous person, is still holding us literally in contempt for protecting our own land from reckless despoilment from outsiders. The justice department and the land claims negotiators are demanding the same thing: that we immediately and irrevocably surrender.

But we will not. Our parents' generation fought against repression hidden behind Pierre Trudeau's icy smile and made important advances for our people. They shook up Ottawa and went to London and New York to demand that Canada respect the human and Indigenous rights of our people. Today, it is going to take an even more intensely fought movement to complete the decolonization of our peoples under the next Trudeau regime.

I listen as the corporate lawyers string together a final series of illegals. Illegal assembly, illegal obstruction, illegal occupation. Then it is over.

The judge, as they so often do in these situations, finds in favour of the mining company.

Injunction granted.

So now, if our youth and Elders go back up to try to protect our Serengeti lands, the Sacred Headwaters region of the Stikine, Nass and Skeena rivers, from another poisonous Imperial Minerals spill, they will be handcuffed and arrested. If they resist, they will be beaten.

That is the equation offered us by the Canadian legal system. We leave the court but we know we will be back again and again until we have the justice that time and again, this legal system denies us.

CHAPTER 33

CRIMINALIZATION OF PROTEST

We will not be waiting idly for Canada to create its justice system.

The new path has been pointed out by Idle No More and Defenders of the Land, organizations that sprung from the grassroots and are completely independent from government and government-funded organizations. They are gradually beginning to change the nearly impossible odds that faced small groups of activists fighting government and industry in isolation.

Idle No More and Defenders of the Land, which came from slightly different traditions but have merged their efforts over the past three years, must continue to remain activist and uncompromising on the issue of our Aboriginal title and rights and remain focused on the land issue. Their strength is that they have proven their ability to mobilize support not only among Indigenous people but among non-Indigenous allies in the environmental, trade union and related social movements. We see how this new grassroots leadership and its allies can push our struggle forward into substantial gains for our peoples on the land question by supporting our Aboriginal title battles and our United Nations recognized right to our lands.

Idle No More and Defenders of the Land stand in solidarity with communities across the country who are defending their lands and their Aboriginal rights. This support is critical because anyone who defends their lands is met with criminalization and repression by security forces and they need help in raising funds to defend themselves, and strong voices that can take their cause to the international level.

The international level is important, because the world has clearly staked out its position on the rights of Indigenous peoples in UNDRIP, and that document forcefully states that we have ownership rights to our lands. If UNDRIP was respected by the Canadian government, we would have no need for barricades. We could meet to discuss how the land might be shared and how it needs to be protected. What we would have on the table would be access and benefits — those are the only issues at question after our title is recognized. But the Trudeau government is refusing to implement UNDRIP and refuses even to respect its own Supreme Court rulings of our proprietary interest in our lands, so we meet instead at the barricades.

It is the existing Canadian strategy to use criminalization, civil action, police repression and other penalties to repress Indigenous resistance to these policies by bringing to bear the weight of the security forces against Indigenous individuals and communities. The use of incarceration is part of a long-term legal strategy that paralyzes communities in lengthy and costly legal proceedings, removing them as obstacles from destructive development on their lands.

In a larger sense, the Crown is conducting a legal-political-fiscal war on First Nations. For evidence, look at the recent media reports of Indigenous and Northern Affairs Canada's "hot spot reporting system" of "Native unrest" operating since 2007. And the inclusion of "radical Indigenous groups" in Canada's draft counterinsurgency manual in 2009 as well as the RCMP's Joint Intelligence Group monitoring threats to "critical infrastructure" by Indigenous bands. Look also at the close collaboration between the oil industry, RCMP and Indigenous and Northern Affairs designed to pacify resistance to the social and ecological devastation of the tar sands.

As late as 2015, a journalist uncovered the existence of the RCMP Project SITKA — a police operation tracking Indigenous activists "who pose a threat to the maintenance of peace and order." It revealed that the police were following eighty-nine activists who met "the criteria for criminality associated to public order events." Project SITKA tracks activists organizing around natural resource development (fighting oil pipelines and shale gas expansion), anti-capitalism (G20 and Occupy activists), the missing and murdered Indigenous women inquiry, Idle No More and land claims. The report concludes that the protesters "pose a criminal threat to Aboriginal public order events," though it concedes that "there is no known evidence that these individuals pose a direct threat to critical infrastructure." This proof of surveillance sent a chill through the activist community. Still, I could not help but smile when I learned that eighty-eight of the names in the document had been blacked out by the Access to Information people and the only name visible was my friend Russell Diabo. That is certainly a badge of honour for him.

SITKA underlines again Canada's insidiousness in using the executive branch and the mainstream criminal justice system to remove Indigenous activists from their land, rather than to bring their policies in line with Canadian judicial decisions, the Canadian Constitution and international law. Idle No More and Defenders of the Land must be prepared to support every community and the individuals who take a stand on our land rights. At the same time, we must cast the net further and bring grassroots Indigenous peoples from across the continent together to fight for political and economic justice.

This is happening today. In the two great environmental battles fought by Native Americans south of the border, the Keystone pipeline fight and the more recent Dakota pipeline battle, Indigenous peoples from north of the border have shown their active support. In the future this can be a powerful alliance in defending Indigenous lands from state and industry incursions throughout Turtle Island.

That is where we are today. I cannot emphasize too often that in our struggle, we must show the same intensity as American blacks did in the 1960s. They had to march in cities across America and they filled up the jails. In Birmingham, when all of the adult protestors were jailed, hundreds of school students took part in the children's crusade, where they marched downtown to talk to the mayor about segregation in their city. The marchers were stopped by the police who brought fire hoses to ward off the children and set police dogs after them. The sight of the southern whites hosing the black youth and siccing dogs on them was the most popular news item in Moscow and around the world that week. In the next city election, all of the segregationists were thrown out. Birmingham was dramatically changed by that incident to the point where it was eventually given an award as the most integrated city in the United States.

Our battle must be as intense as the fight against racism in the American south and against apartheid in South Africa. Self-determination on our traditional lands is the only solution to colonialism. Canadians must realize that we have to build a new Canada, a whole new country based on recognition of our Aboriginal and treaty rights — a Canada that recognizes our right to self-determination and our land rights in Section 35 of the Constitution. We as leaders and human rights advocates have an important role in educating Canada about what a new country can be. But finally it will come from the grassroots, when we give our people the tools they need to make the change they need. They will block environmental disasters like the Red Chris Mine from destroying our lands, and pipelines from carrying the oil and bitumen that is destroying our climate, as they are doing today. They will stand their ground on our own land and send out their message for solidarity to the world.

CHAPTER 34

NON-VIOLENCE, BUT NOT PASSIVE ACCEPTANCE

We arrive at the question of violence — the ostensible reason the RCMP is doing their surveillance on Russ and the other eighty-eight unnamed activists in Project SITKA, and countless other surveillance operations against us. In Canada, if you challenge the status quo, if you urge people to stand their ground and stand up for their rights, you will be asked, generally in ominous tones, if you are "advocating violence."

My first instinct is to point out that the overwhelming and unrelenting source of violence in relations between Indigenous and non-Indigenous peoples has come from the settler state, but I don't, because I know that my earnest interlocutor will instantly assume that, yes indeed, I am indirectly advocating anti-Canadian violence!

Well, I can assure you that I am not.

There is no question that in Canada non-violence is the only way for Indigenous peoples to achieve self-determination. But this does not mean we will not create tension within the existing colonial system. Creating tension is not only unavoidable, it is essential to bring about change. There is indeed a difference and no one expressed this better than

Martin Luther King, Jr. in his Letter from Birmingham Jail:

> Nonviolent direct action seeks to create
> such a crisis and foster such a tension that
> a community which has constantly refused
> to negotiate is forced to confront the issue.
> It seeks so to dramatize the issue that it
> can no longer be ignored. My citing the
> creation of tension as part of the work of
> the nonviolent resister may sound rather
> shocking. But I must confess that I am
> not afraid of the word "tension." I have
> earnestly opposed violent tension, but there
> is a type of constructive, nonviolent tension
> which is necessary for growth . . . we see
> the need for nonviolent gadflies to create
> the kind of tension in society that will help
> men rise from the dark depths of prejudice
> and racism to the majestic heights of under-
> standing and brotherhood.

In Canada, we are still far from those "majestic heights." To understand why creating tension is necessary you have to look at how our opponents normalized the theft of our lands in the first place. The British were superb at taking over places based on shuffling papers and filling out documents — then sending out overwhelming military forces to defend their "legal" title to other people's land. Our Indigenous leaders in the Interior realized this more than a hundred years ago. In 1910, the Interior chiefs wrote the Laurier Memorial, protesting the usurpation of their lands because they realized that the British were stealing their land on paper. The Indigenous peoples of that time had never seen the Constitution of Canada or the maps the white people made for themselves, but they recognized that somehow the land was being stolen out from underneath them and they wanted this to stop. So they wrote their own account of the step-by-step white invasion of our territories and they submitted this to Prime Minister Laurier in protest.

This paper-pushing all seems very abstract but it is important to understand that in colonial jurisdiction, behind all of the maps, licences, government surveys and land use regulations, there is always some bureaucrat responsible for every square inch of Aboriginal and treaty territory. They want you to get a permit or permission to do anything you do on their responsibility area or they will get an injunction and enforcement order to have you removed. This basically means you do not need to do anything except show up on any unoccupied or disputed area and set up camp and you will sooner or later be visited by the colonial authorities. I am saying this simply to explain that taking any kind of action out in your territory will have an impact. It will not necessarily be splashed across the news, but when you are exercising your right to self-determination, you are challenging them.

The old colonial structure and decision-making process is so entrenched in Canada that Prime Minster Harper said we do not have colonialism in Canada. This means that we do need to exercise self-determination across this country to get these little colonial bureaucrats to understand that there are new decision makers coming back onto the scene. The business-as-usual strategy of the federal and provincial governments is a strategy they use but it is not law. It is, in fact, contrary to the obligation that international human rights treaties and the Constitution demand from the federal and provincial governments.

The business-as-usual strategy is really callous and humiliating. It means that they know we have been so socially and economically marginalized, so impoverished, that even though we do actually have legally recognized rights, they do not give a damn. They are going to carry on business as usual and push us out of the way because they are strong and we are weak. This is very much like the situation in the US in the 1830s, when the Supreme Court Chief Justice John Marshall ruled that Indigenous peoples within the country's borders had sovereign rights and the lawful title to their lands. But President Andrew Jackson shrugged off their rights and the jurisdiction of his own Supreme Court by saying, "John Marshall has made his decision; now let him enforce it!" Jackson then carried out ethnic cleansing on the Cherokee people from all of their lands east of the Mississippi river in the infamous Trail of Tears.

Similarly, business as usual in Canada says that Indigenous peoples are too inferior to demand equality and self-determination. We have been marginalized over the last 150 years, so now it is actually emotionally stressful for us to assert our equality. Especially when the courts and the police are at the barricades saying, you actually have no right to be equal at all. That is when violence can erupt even though it is a peaceful demonstration. Violence is something we should never initiate or wish for. In fact, watch carefully. You will see that almost always, violence comes from the state because that, after all, is how they keep us in check. We must never initiate violence ourselves, but at the same time we should never go quietly. We stand our ground.

And for that we need to support our Warriors. The road to self-determination has to include training and organization of our Warriors to protect our peoples and our rights. These forces have to be developed under our own governments and not be extensions of the forces that are designed to protect the old status quo.

I know that even in some of our own communities, Warriors are looked at with suspicion in peaceful times. But when Aboriginal and treaty rights run into conflict with federal or provincial laws, and the Warriors, often our young women and men, stand up for the people and their rights, they are quickly elevated in importance. Our Warriors at the barricades have to be strong and smart and hold their emotions in check when they fight back — always create an environment that allows for change instead of violence, which will only serve to entrench the status quo.

Warriors are important because we need the capacity to protect and defend our Aboriginal and treaty rights. A responsible Warrior Society that is properly trained and connected to the local Indigenous people's grassroots decision-making power structure is essential for establishing ourselves and for protecting our Aboriginal title and rights into the future.

The RCMP and national security officers are committed to the old colonial model of decision making in Canada. They follow the precedent set out by decisions that saw colonial rule as sacred and Indigenous peoples as excess baggage. I also know that the RCMP and national security officers have infiltrated our organizations and will use these infiltrators for information to convict us and, very often, as agents provocateurs who try to incite violence, which they can use to isolate us and give the green light to the RCMP, provincial police or army to violently oppress us. Violence is the game of our oppressor. Our response is non-violent resistance.

But we should never be afraid of creating tension in our struggles. We must stand up to our oppressors and, while no one in their right mind would seek it, we should not be afraid of going to jail. Creating tension is the only means to decolonize ourselves because the colonized in Canada are accustomed to treating Indigenous peoples as non-human beings.

We want to build a new Canada based on the *Constitution Act, 1982* and stop Canada and the provinces from carrying on business as usual under the outdated *BNA Act* division of powers, where only the federal and provincial governments have law-making powers.

Our Aboriginal title and rights, and our right to self-determination as recognized in the UN Covenant and the UN Declaration of the Rights of Indigenous Peoples, must be recognized by Canada and the world. We must never accept less and we must be prepared to fight for our rights anywhere and everywhere they are challenged.

Finally, on the question of violence, we should really turn it around. In equally ominous tones we should ask our interlocutors if they are advocating or condoning violence against us.

Because in fact, they surely do. It is the first response of all settler states. From the papal bull of the fifteenth century to the present it has been their guiding principle and the source of their power. Ours must be non-violent resistance. Fierce resistance.

CHAPTER 35
RESISTING THE CARBON BOMB

The main impediment to Canada's dirty energy market is the fact that Indigenous peoples hold constitutionally protected title and rights to their lands, with which industry and government must legally comply.

This is not just an economic issue. Indigenous peoples are very concerned about Canada's dirty energy policy. We believe that the oil and gas industry has had its day and the pipelines — far from being expanded — should be gradually turned off. Today's oil profits should not be directed to the 1 per cent, but should be invested into alternative energy solutions.

When I state these things, people might think that I am pretending to be some kind of environmental angel. The fact is, I have myself earned a living off oil and gas. I know what it's about. But there is a time when you have to pull a plug on something when you see it is doing harm and today scientists the world over have proven that the oil and gas industry is doing terrible harm to our atmosphere. And, as I saw when I toured the tar sands, terrible harm on the ground. The tar sands are a disaster for the people of the region and, when it is extracted and burned in the air, for people and animals everywhere on the planet.

Indigenous peoples have to use all of their strength to close down the global warming threats to themselves and to Mother Earth. We see clearly that Justin Trudeau is our enemy in this. In September 2016, his environment minister, Catherine McKenna, flanked by the minister of national resources and B.C. Premier Christy Clark, stood at the Sea Island Coast Guard base outside of Vancouver to approve the $36 billion Pacific NorthWest Liquefied Natural Gas pipeline that had been fiercely opposed by environmentalists and Indigenous land protectors. But because this was a Trudeau government minister, the announcement had to be made with a scattershot of lies, among them her contention that the approval was based on both the "best available science and on Indigenous traditional knowledge."

If built, Pacific NorthWest LNG, which is owned by the Malaysian government, will be one of the largest carbon polluters in the country and a serious obstacle to Canada living up to its climate commitments. Matt Horne of the Pembina Institute pointed out that "the project will involve scaling up fracking in northeastern B.C., building a pipeline to the West Coast and constructing an export terminal on Lelu Island, near a crucial area for juvenile salmon." In all, the Pacific NorthWest LNG project is expected to emit 9.2 million tonnes of carbon dioxide equivalent annually — equal to 1.9 million cars — into the atmosphere. "By 2050," Horne says, "the entire province of B.C. is supposed to emit 13 million tonnes of carbon pollution. With LNG line approval alone, meeting the climate target becomes an impossibility."

For his part, Grand Chief Stewart Phillip was not impressed by the "Indigenous traditional knowledge" that went into the project. "The LNG project would obliterate the Skeena River sockeye run in B.C. Clearly we have grave concerns about this project."

Stewart also looked at what the decision had done to the faith of Indigenous peoples in the Trudeau government. "What is at risk here is the rapidly deteriorating relationship between the Indigenous people that came out in unprecedented numbers, being inspired by the promises and commitments made by Mr. Trudeau during the last federal election. We are now moving," he said, "toward a very conflictual relationship with the Trudeau government."

CARBON BOMB 2

That relationship between B.C. Indigenous peoples and the Trudeau government became even more contentious two months later when the Trudeau government announced they were approving the Kinder Morgan pipeline, which passes through hundreds of kilometres of Secwepemc traditional territory, crossing and in some places criss-crossing the main salmon rivers and passing through our most precious and environmentally sensitive areas. Two days before the announcement, I had sent the prime minister an open letter as head of INET and with the support of my band, and friend Chief Judy Wilson. I include the full text here because it provides a summary of what we, as Indigenous peoples in general and as Secwepemc people in particular, are up against in the Kinder Morgan pipeline.

OPEN LETTER REGARDING THE PROPOSED KINDER MORGAN TRANS MOUNTAIN PIPELINE EXPANSION THROUGH SECWEPEMC TERRITORY

Dear Right Honourable Prime Minister Justin Trudeau,

I am writing you as the Spokesperson of the Indigenous Network on Economies and Trade (INET) and a member of the Secwepemc Nation in regard to the Kinder Morgan Expansion through Secwepemc Territory. Secwepemcúl'ecw, the land on which we live, eat, sustain our culture, practice our ceremonies, and exercise our rights, is the largest Indigenous territory that the Kinder Morgan Trans Mountain Pipeline expansion would cross — passing through 518 kilometres of our territory.

I would like to remind you that this pipeline requires the consent of the Secwepemc people. We do not accept that the federal government can make this decision unilaterally and without the prior informed consent of the Secwepemc people as the rightful titleholders. Kinder Morgan has signed deals with a few Indian Band Councils[1] but neither the band councils nor Kinder Morgan have engaged with the Secwepemc people as the rightful titleholders. These agreements can only be made on behalf of their status as federal Indian Bands and do not represent the rightful titleholders. In fact,

---

1. With the Simpcw, the Tk'emlups te Secwepemc and Whispering Pines Indian Bands. The only consultations with the Secwepemc people have been through the NEB process and the ministerial panel, both fatally flawed processes that failed to properly take into account our collectively held Aboriginal title and rights.

the agreements are made with Bands whose reserves cover less than 1 per cent of the Secwepemc Territory along the existing Kinder Morgan Pipeline and they appear to be little more than cynical attempts to divide and conquer our people — as we have seen on so many other occasions.[2]

In response, INET, along with a group of concerned Secwepemc people, has undertaken to organize a broad based action we are calling STOP for "Secwepemc Trans-mountain Oversight Plenary." The purpose of this Plenary is to gather on the land in the spring of 2017 to discuss and decide on Kinder Morgan expansion through the Secwepemc Territory and then to collectively determine on a course of action.

According to Secwepemc, Canadian, and international law, title and rights are vested in the Secwepemc people as a whole. It is only by starting with our traditional land users and stewards — those who exercise the right to hunt, fish, gather, and practice our culture — that we can truly understand the impacts of the pipeline and achieve this level of engagement. The STOP plenary will gather their perspectives on the proposed pipeline. It is these members of our nation who will feel the impacts of the pipeline on our rights and our food sovereignty most acutely. The pipeline weaves through some of our most important water

---

2. This tactic that has been condemned by the world. Most recently, Anastasia Crickley, Chair of the UN Committee on the Elimination of Racial Discrimination (CERD) who questioned Canada in a October 3, 2016, letter about using "divide and rule strategies" within the Secwepemc Nation when attempting to negotiate a land claims agreement through the British Columbia treaty process.

systems, threatening the Thompson River system which is connected to the Adams River, which is a vital spawning habitat for chinook, coho, and pink salmon, and home one of the most important sockeye runs in the world. We have yet to hear from our land users on the impacts the pipeline could have on our salmon, our food sovereignty, and our rights as Secwepemc people.

Any leakage would immediately threaten the pacific salmon who spawn in the Thompson and Fraser River basins. It is not surprising that most Secwepemc people are in complete solidarity with the Water Protectors from Standing Rock North Dakota. Our waters are also sacred. The salmon and the rivers they inhabit have taken care of our people for centuries and we are obligated as Secwepemc people to protect the Thompson River system for future generations.

We also take seriously the issue of climate change and wonder how you could possibly give approval to this pipeline if you yourself are serious about transition to a low carbon industry. Canada cannot afford and does not need any expansion in pipeline capacity and further GHG emissions if we hope to reduce the current damage to the planet.

I am attaching a map outlining the boundaries of Secwepemc Territory which the existing Kinder Morgan pipeline bisects, with the proposed Kinder Morgan Trans Mountain Expansion along the same route. It is important to point out that the first Kinder Morgan pipeline was not approved by the Secwepemc people because we were outlawed under the *Indian Act* from organizing around our land rights from 1926–1951. Canada appears to want to ignore us again.

Nevertheless, Canada is obliged to seek the consent of Indigenous peoples on the Kinder Morgan Trans Mountain Expansion under its international human and Indigenous rights obligations.

The Secwepemc people convening the Plenary on Kinder Morgan Trans Mountain Expansion will keep your office apprised of our decision after we gather together on the land in the spring of 2017. We expect Canada not to proceed with any approvals or decisions regarding the proposed Kinder Morgan Trans Mountain Expansion until hearing from the Secwepemc people on this matter.

Yours truly,
Arthur Manuel

The approval of Kinder Morgan two days later was the second gravest criminal act Justin has committed — after the abandonment of the international declaration of our rights in UNDRIP. And they are not unrelated. He had to abrogate UNDRIP to give himself a free hand to build pipelines across our territories. Because he knew that if UNDRIP is properly implemented, he would need not just to "consult" Indigenous peoples, he would have to gain our consent. And that, he knows, we will never give.

Our job now is to show him that we cannot so easily be swept aside and preparations are underway for our people to gather on our land in the spring of 2017 and decide our own fate.

CHAPTER 36

DEFENDING
MOTHER EARTH

In defending the land at this time of the international global warming crisis, we are defending something much larger than Indigenous rights. Our fight today is to preserve the planet in a livable form.

Every year the earth sets new records for warming — the climate disaster that we have been warned about is here and we will have to take dramatic action if we are to avert the worst consequences. A recent study in the journal *Nature* has shown that, globally, 33 per cent of all known oil reserves must be left in the ground if the world is to keep within the already dangerous 2 degree temperature increase. The study's conclusion on the exploitation of Canada's oil sands was unequivocal. Production must fall to "negligible" levels after 2020 if the 2 degree scenario is to be fulfilled. The research also finds no climate-friendly scenario in which any oil or gas is drilled in the Arctic.

These studies underscore the fact that Trudeau and his gang in Ottawa are really climate deniers, or at the very least climate liars, in their insistence that they can continue for decades on end to drain oil from the oil sands and still stay within acceptable climate limits. In insisting on bringing the oil sands to market, Prime Minister Trudeau is committing intergenerational warfare against my children and grand-children, as he is with his own.

Indigenous peoples have a real responsibility to fight against the petro-politics that is driving Canada's estab-lishment, and for a clean energy policy that will leave a livable future for our children. It is our responsibility to promote our Indigenous concept of economy to replace the Eurocentric form that is destroying our environment. We need to find our voice in this discussion, or we will wind up getting solutions from greenwashing strategies that are not really green, but just another way big business makes money pretending to address this problem. The greenwashers are trying to run an environmental scam against Mother Earth and we know that she cannot be fooled.

When the Europeans first came to North America five hundred years ago, Europe looked at the natural wealth of our territories and claimed we did not know how to use our land, so they claimed it under the colonial doctrines of discovery and colonized us. This meant they dispos-sessed us of our land, made us dependent upon them and oppressed us when we resisted. Now our lands have been seriously depleted. But they continue high grading oil and fracking natural gas while at the same time pretending to be concerned about dirty energy problems and global warming. You cannot have it both ways. You either commit yourself to a clean energy policy or not. Trudeau and his tricksters never miss a chance to speak glowingly of clean energy while at the same time devoting all of their energies and energy policies to ensuring the continued dominance of dirty energy. This fact was hidden in plain sight when they were in opposition, when they criticized the Harper government for not having "social licence" for their energy extraction and transportation blitz. Once in power, the Liberals tried to get "social licence" with small meaningless concessions and lofty words with the intention of using that licence to implement, almost unchanged, the aggressive and environmentally disastrous "energy superpower" policies of Stephen Harper. Now that more and more people are pointing this out about Trudeau and publicly denouncing his policies, his government has suddenly become silent over social licence while they make dark hints of using the army to quell resistance to the expansion of the country's fossil fuel infrastructure.

This channelling of the spirit of Stephen Harper in Justin Trudeau is obvious in my Secwepemc territory where Trudeau approved the Kinder Morgan pipeline.

Grassroots Indigenous peoples challenge the continuing reckless and destructive industry invasion of our territories, despite the fact that we are financially poor, because we know ultimately we will be poorer if we let them destroy the land and poison the air. We still live off the land, so our laws are based on respecting Mother Earth because it is Mother Earth that gives life. We challenge Canada, the provinces and industry to protect Mother Earth, and we are the real driving force behind the environmental movement because we still depend on her for our food, medicine and our spiritual life. Our values, language and culture give us strength to fight this David and Goliath struggle, and none of our people are fooled by the Liberal government rhetoric.

We know that the expenses we are charging to Mother Earth are being put on our grandchildren's credit card. Do not believe the scam artists who are saying that a mine will not damage your watershed or that a pipeline is leak proof. Mines do damage watersheds and all pipelines eventually leak.

Aboriginal and treaty rights are a counterbalance to the stranglehold petro-politics and the resource extraction industry has on Canada and the provinces. It is our duty to address global warming and other related environmental problems Canada needs to face up to. We, as Indigenous peoples, need to use our power to protect Mother Earth not only for our own good but for the good of all humanity.

A QUESTION OF VALUES

It is obvious that Indigenous peoples are threatened by mining and pipeline activity in Canada so it is critical that Indigenous peoples, and not just the leaders, get acquainted with the impacts mining and pipelines are going to have on our lives. Federal and provincial governments want to keep all the fundamental decisions on access and benefit sharing within their federal and provincial law-making powers. They do not want to share decision making and benefits with Indigenous peoples. Instead, they will try to limit Indigenous involvement to jobs, token business opportunities and revenue sharing.

The Canadian and provincial governments are trying to challenge any opposition to the mining and pipeline industry by investing in employment strategies to get Indigenous peoples to work for the pipeline and mining industry. But pipelines and mining industries are very dirty industries and we have a responsibility to make our own pipeline and mining policies and laws according to our own values. Traditionally, Indigenous peoples' economies have always been based on clean energy and making a minimum impact on animals, land, water and air.

Of course jobs, economic opportunities and revenue sharing should be part of the basis of any economic relationship with Indigenous peoples, but they can never be traded for Aboriginal title and rights. The real negotiations must be based on the broader economic matters like dirty energy policies versus clean energy policies; wild salmon conservation and fish farms; clear cut and selective logging and mining exploration and environmental mitigation. Aboriginal title and rights are dependent upon a clean and natural habitat.

Indigenous peoples are accustomed to thinking about the impact human activities will have on our future generations. This is part of our spiritual relationship with our traditional territories and this is really our qualification for addressing these economic matters.

The mining industry and the pipeline promoters are going to put a lot of pressure on the chiefs and councils in our territory and they are used to ignoring and overriding Indigenous values and principles under the colonial system. Indigenous peoples should never feel pressured to change our values because these values can protect the earth for everyone.

CHAPTER 37
THE LONG-TERM APPROACH

As I write this, I can hear our critics saying: "But we can't simply oppose all development!"

It is the universal refrain from those who never want to oppose any development.

So I will state clearly that we do not oppose all development on our lands. But we do oppose irresponsible development. All we ask is that any development be fully measured in terms of the cost and benefits they will have not only for us but for our children, grandchildren and future generations. We should not simply look at quick cash to cover off existing deficits or top up salaries for jobs the government is cutting back on. I know we are in a big money crunch right now. In fact, so is the province of B.C. because they mismanaged the forestry and fisheries in our territory. I know that mining and water are now on their planning table and I know they will mismanage these resources too.

I know Canada and B.C. are committed to a dirty energy policy because they are willing to pipe dirty oil through our territory. They are addicted to oil and gas like an alcoholic is addicted to booze. This fossil fuel addiction also carries over to minerals. We are destroying our land and water for minerals that really have no real benefit or that actively harm us, like mining for microscopic gold or minerals that poison the air.

We need to measure all industrial resource activities by their true and full impact on not only our air and water, but also on our culture and values. As Indigenous peoples we view all human activity with the understanding that water, land, animals, plants, fish and human beings are equal. We understand that if we damage one area it will eventually impact us. Human beings do not dominate the earth, but are part of the earth. This is very different than the economic values of the Europeans.

Only recently has the value of the natural world begun to creep into the European concept of economics. Originally the environment was considered an externality, which means it was not factored into the cost of business. That meant that the business did not have to pay for the damage it did to the water and land. Instead, the environmental degradation and destruction was covered by society and the government. Society had to live with poisoned water created by businesses or pay to clean it up. This is just now beginning to change, and we need to understand how we can make these changes work for us — or at least help to protect us in the short term.

An important part of this change is included in the legal requirement imposed on the federal and provincial governments to seek and achieve consultation and accommodation with Indigenous peoples. And much more specifically is the UNDRIP demand that our free prior informed consent is required before there can be any development on our land. This puts us in a very critical position to help Canada and the world to make adjustments that will at long last free us from our fossil fuel addiction. We can use our responsibility to protect Mother Earth as part of our contribution to the modern environmental struggle and this, in turn, will help us win a broader base of support for our Aboriginal and treaty rights.

Those bands who do not assert their rights and instead sit down with the government to negotiate them away are being very short-sighted — and they impact all of us. They make us all look like we are on the one hand as money-obsessed as Europeans, and on the other easily cheated because the money we ask for is a mere fraction of percentage of the overall wealth taken from our land. We have been marginalized for so many decades that we do not really understand how governments and industry allocate and divide up the benefits from our land.

So when development passes the test of sustainability over many generations, we can allow it in our territories and at that point we should be fairly compensated for rights to our own resources. Then it is also essential that a significant part of those profits are allocated to ongoing environmental protection and research projects, so we can ensure a clean and sustainable planet for our children and grandchildren.

These are the kind of arrangements that must be looked at by the rightful title holders and, if implemented, they should also be monitored by them. We should not limit ourselves to short-term jobs, business opportunities and quick-buck revenue sharing. We need to use our economic power to give full meaning to our sovereignty and self-determination and, most important, to protecting our lands for future generations.

CHAPTER 38

DECLARING SOVEREIGNTY ON THE GROUND

Here it is important to give a caveat. When we speak of asserting our rights on the ground, it is a very profound step and one thing we must avoid is making grand declarations of sovereignty and then following it up with . . . nothing. This is not only useless, it is profoundly injurious to our cause.

I know it feels great for Indigenous peoples to dramatically declare their sovereignty but what it means on the ground depends on how you back up your words with your deeds. I know this from countless struggles where our people literally had to fight off the settler security forces of the day. I also experienced how struggles on the ground divided our nation between those who wanted to negotiate and those who wanted to fight it out. I am therefore always interested in seeing how far a group of establishment leaders and institutions are prepared to fight for their sovereignty on the ground before I move to join them.

The government is always talking about the "strength of claim" in determining how seriously they will take any Indigenous claim to our territory. The establishment groups should get support for their position among the people before making their claims. It takes a massive movement to have our sovereignty recognized on the ground. I think the constitutional and legal foundation is there. I think, generally speaking, many Canadians are interested in dealing with this issue if we ourselves can approach it in an organized way.

The real problem is that we lack leadership to get this done. We actually are sending mixed signals to industry and government. On the one hand, some of our Indian bands sign Reconciliation Framework Agreements. On the other, the same band also declares Aboriginal title and rights to specific areas of their territory. In signing the Reconciliation Agreements, they are handing over their title to the provincial government and industry so when, in the next breath, they declare sovereignty, it sounds confusing and makes us look inconsistent and, to be honest, a bit simple-minded.

If we are going to be taken seriously, especially when we declare our title and rights to our territory, we better be consistent in our strategy and refuse to sign any agreement that offers or implies the surrender of our rights. The Indian bands that have never signed the provincial government agreements are in a far better political position to declare Aboriginal title over their territories. What is being challenged is who has underlying title to our territory. Does underlying title belong to the Indigenous peoples or does it belong to the Crown — that is always the crux of the matter and we have to be absolutely consistent in our answer to the question.

The important question is, will these Indian bands back up their declaration or will they just let the province carry on business as usual? If that happens, then they will make our position weaker instead of stronger because they will be saying, on one hand, we assert our Aboriginal title and rights, and on the other hand, don't worry, it doesn't actually mean anything.

Finally, we need to be very concerned about some of our leaders using these kinds of declarations to merely trade-off for a bigger surrender settlement than they would get otherwise. This is in fact what many of our deal-making leaders do. They claim Aboriginal title and rights and then immediately throw them down on the negotiating table. They are not in the business of asserting our rights, but of selling them.

Regardless of what you think about this strategy and about the leadership that is promoting it, we will be affected by these false declarations. We need to take them seriously and to put some thought into all of their implications before making the great intoxicating pronouncements of sovereignty and waking up the next day with nothing to show for it but a hangover and some embarrassing memories.

CHAPTER 39

STANDING WITH STANDING ROCK

One of the most promising new developments in recent years are the new alliances north and south of the Medicine Line.

It was a freezing December day when I arrived in Standing Rock, but there were still thousands of people camped out at the main camp. I was there representing the Seventh Generation Fund for Indigenous Peoples — an organization that I am a board member of — and I was pleased to see the Secwepemc flag flapping in the wind in the row of Indigenous flags along the main road. It was there because of the solidarity between many of the grassroots Secwepemc and the Sioux of Standing Rock. Many of our people came to show their support, and the water protectors opposing the Dakota Access pipeline have promised to return the favour in helping us in our fight against the Kinder Morgan pipeline expansion through our territory.

Despite the icy temperatures and the fact that the camp was encircled by para-militaries, I had a good time at Standing Rock, meeting with people from the Spiritual, Warrior and tribal groups. They have gathered around them a very dynamic and powerful group of Indigenous and non-Indigenous activists, committed to fighting against the black snake — as they refer to the pipeline. Among them, I was happy to run into Naomi Klein, a long-time friend and political inspiration who also wrote the foreword to *Unsettling Canada*. She too had come to show her solidarity and to bring attention to the importance of the fight against the pipelines that were bringing to market far more oil than our planet can safely burn.

I also arrived the same day as US veterans who had come to protect the protectors after the violent attacks on them by the para-military police during the fall. This is something new in our battles, with Indigenous peoples on the front lines against the state and the resource extractors that they represent, being joined by broad sections of the larger society. In the Keystone battle, it was a coalition of "Cowboys and Indians" with the local ranchers joining Indigenous peoples and environmentalists in combatting the destructive forces of runaway development. We also saw this in Canada in Elsipogtog, when local people who were equally concerned about the effect of fracking on their drinking water quietly joined the Mi'kmaq-led blockade.

But once again it is a complex battle. The same issues we are confronted with north of the Medicine Line, the division that often arises between the people and their establishment leaders, were visible at Standing Rock. The fight is led by the water protectors, and the band council often acts like band councils in Canada, ready to settle for a small sum of money and a promise of a handful of jobs — rather than stand up and fight for its rights and the community's long-term health. Our situation is similar. Kamloops, North Thompson and Whispering Pines have signed deals with the Kinder Morgan pipeline. Indian bands can, of course, do what they want, but Secwepemc territory belongs to the Secwepemc people collectively. Band councils have jurisdiction on the postage stamp–sized lands set aside under the *Indian Act*, but it is the whole nation that holds collective title to our vast national territories.

In Standing Rock, there was real tension between the band council and the water protectors. This is part of life and we have to deal with it. The fact that all women do not stand together with the women's movement in no way diminishes its extraordinary and transformative importance today and over the past fifty years. This is the same with all movements. Even Martin Luther King, Jr. had countless critics and obstructers among US establishment blacks. So the fact that all Indigenous people do not stand together in no way diminishes the power of our movement. The fact is, some who are born into our groups do not share our values, often because their life experiences have diverged from ours — and they do not want to share our collective struggle. That is their right but it does not mean that we in any way have to dilute our commitment. Others, born into other groups, stand with us. And they add to our strength.

Governments, of course, thrive in exploiting any division they can find. In Canada, the prime minster and Kinder Morgan will suggest that the signatures of the three Shuswap chiefs who are ready to do a deal is good enough, because it serves their interests to suggest this. After all, a lot of big investors have pumped billions and billions of dollars into the tar sands and they need to sell their dirty oil in Asia to recoup their investment and make a profit. So if they can work their neocolonial black magic behind closed doors with three chiefs who are on their payroll, they will.

This is how neocolonialism worked in the past. This is how it still works today.

But we will be there to remind them that when the first Kinder Morgan pipeline went through our territory in the early 1950s, we were not consulted and we never gave our approval. We were actually prohibited by the *Indian Act* to meet and talk about our land rights from 1926 to 1951, so it would have been illegal for us to even consider a position on the pipeline.

But the 1950s are long gone. Today, the province of B.C. needs to get the permission of the Secwepemc Nation and not just the local Indian bands located along the Kinder Morgan pipeline if it wants to build a new line through our territory. We will remind them that the Supreme Court of Canada was very clear in stating that Aboriginal title and rights are a collective right and not a "federal Indian band right." The court made it clear that Indigenous people are the rightful title holders and not the band.

While Kinder Morgan has signed deals with the Simpcw, Whispering Pines and Kamloops Indian bands chiefs, those three Indian bands do not represent the nation. The three bands do have the right to sign a deal for how Kinder Morgan does specifically affect them, but they cannot sign on behalf of the Secwepemc Nation. Canada, British Columbia and Kinder Morgan cannot legitimately build the second pipeline and get direct economic benefit from using Secwepemc territory to convey energy to the global marketplace.

When I spoke to the Standing Rock assembly, I told them that I, along with the people I represent, am committed to no more pipelines. I said our governments cannot logically say we are going to stop carbon

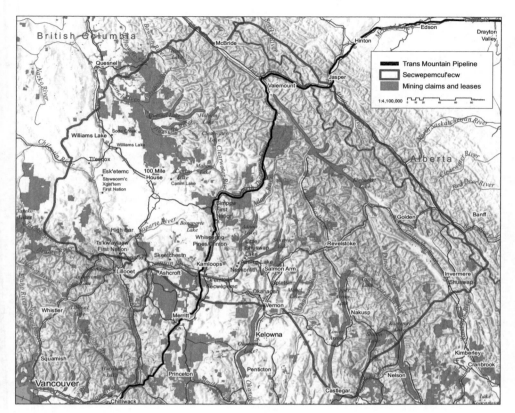

The proposed Kinder Morgan Trans Mountain Pipeline snakes through more than 500 kilometres of our territory.

emissions and at the same time build more pipelines. I said that Dakota Access pipeline was plan B for the failed Keystone pipeline. And that the planned Kinder Morgan pipeline through my people's territory is plan B for the failed Gateway pipeline. I told them that just like they felt a duty to stop Dakota Access, the Secwepemc people feel an obligation to protect Mother Earth from the Kinder Morgan pipeline.

I spent several more days at the camp and I had a growing feeling that we are entering a new era. With the election of President Donald Trump, battle lines are being sharply drawn. Positions are hardening and the battle will be long and tough. But on our side, we are increasing our forces.

When I left Standing Rock, another blizzard was moving in. But the Secwepemc flag was still flying with the other Indigenous flags along the entrance to the camp. As I was leaving, I was thanked by local activists for coming to show solidarity. And they promised that if the Kinder Morgan pipeline enters one inch of our territory without our permission, they would come up to stand alongside us to block it. That is the type of promise we can build our victory on.

CHAPTER 40
DEATH OF A WARRIOR

On March 22, 2016, the Secwepemc people lost one of their greatest warriors. Wolverine (William Jones Ignace), was eighty-four years old when he died. He had been a strong supporter of my father in his day and of our land battles everywhere. He rose to special prominence during the unprecedented state violence launched against our people in 1995, the so-called Gustafsen Lake stand-off.

Called Ts'peten in our language, Gustafsen Lake is one of our sacred sites that was being used as grazing land by a local rancher. When the rancher tried to force a group of Sundancers off our land by destroying their camp, the call went for defenders. Among the first to arrive was Wolverine and what unfolded at Ts'peten was a classic example of how the state machinery works. As soon as the land protectors arrived and stood their ground with the rancher, the NDP government in Victoria sent in the RCMP to arrest the Sundancers and "restore order."

The defenders did not back down. Over the next thirty-one days, the RCMP amassed four hundred Emergency Response Team officers complete with armoured personnel carriers. They fired more than seven thousand rounds at the defenders, blew up one of their pickup trucks with a land mine and engaged in propaganda against the Indigenous people there that even one of their PR officers later described as a "smear campaign." Over the next month, the Sundancers were variously described as being members of a cult, as common criminals and, finally, as terrorists.

During the standoff, there were several pitched gun battles. It seems a miracle that no one was killed and only a few on each side were lightly wounded. But the barrage of racist attacks in the press and from the police and government officials continued before and after the firefights.

The standoff ended with a surrender of the camp on September 11, 1995, after visits from spiritual leaders. Almost all who remained were arrested and charged. Wolverine, who had been given a high media profile during the standoff, was given an eight-year sentence and he served a full five years before he was paroled. One of the defenders managed to escape to the US and it is indicative of the outrageous behaviour of Canada's security forces that he sought and was awarded political asylum when an American judge heard the story of Canada's behaviour in the standoff. In a truly strange twist of fate that I still cannot fully understand, but has only added to Wolverine's legend, the RCMP, the people who were shooting at Wolverine, actually awarded him a medallion for courage under fire.

Wolverine left prison unimpressed with the RCMP gesture and more determined than ever to continue the fight for sovereignty. Over the years, he would travel to Europe to address the international community and into southern Mexico to meet with the Zapatistas. All the while he insisted on Secwepemc sovereignty and refused to accept the role of the Canadian state in our lives.

What was less known about Wolverine outside of our community is the Nourish the Nation Garden that he cultivated in his later years. All alone, well into his eighties, he cultivated eight acres of tomatoes, beans, squash, carrots, potatoes and melons, all using traditional organic methods. He gave the food away to those in need, while also making sure that those who were protesting the illegal expansion of outsiders onto our lands always had food in their camps.

In this, again, he was showing us the traditional way. He grew up in the 1930s, before the band administration had welfare to distribute, and at the time our peoples were self-sufficient, growing all kinds of food crops on our reserve. Back then the chief did not have welfare cheques to give out but instead checked to make sure your winter supply was sufficient to take care of your family. If it wasn't, he would express his displeasure and insist you and your family go out and gather more food or firewood — whatever you were short of. I remember Elder and friend Mary Thomas saying everyone used to be a little afraid of Chief Neskonlith because he was a stern man when he assessed your food supply, and was quite insistent in the fall that you go out and amass more to ensure your family could get through even the longest and most bitter winter. We certainly did share our wealth back then, but we were also responsible for taking care of our family and ourselves first.

We did not, as some would have it, put necessities in a common supply depot with everyone taking what they wanted. No, we generated our own food supply and were responsible for taking care of ourselves. We shared what we or our families did not need or traded, for example, for more berries if we did not have enough and we had extra dry fish. This was why we divided our land by family into Certificates of Possession when the reserves were set up. Every family back then had a parcel of land that they put seed to and we had a Water Boss who would schedule our water use. Back then it was flood irrigation and everyone was desperate to get water, especially when it was hot and dry.

Today, many of our people live on social assistance, and I know we can produce all our own food to relieve that economic pressure point. That was what Wolverine was trying to prove when, as an old Warrior, he farmed that eight-acre garden. He wanted his children and grandchildren to learn that you can become independent by growing your own food. We have the land, we have the irrigation system, we just need the planning to use that land to become more self-sufficient. We need the white man's welfare system to be thrown in the garbage. We need to develop our own mixed economy where income generating activity is married to a self-sufficient farming, hunting, fishing and gathering plan, with a place for very carefully planned and managed developments. As Wolverine explained to us in his words and showed us by his example:

> You need two hands to fight the system. You cannot have one hand asking for something. You have to be able to fight with both hands.

In this, he was not only one of our greatest warriors, he was one of our greatest teachers.

PART 8
RE-ENVISIONING CANADA

CHAPTER 41
OUR INALIENABLE RIGHTS

Here, finally, is where we have landed.

As Indigenous peoples, we are the original humans in our territories. In our own languages we call ourselves some version of the people of the land. Our names tell us where we come from. We have inherited our land from our ancestors and we have the responsibility to govern our territories. Our political and legal status as Indigenous peoples obviously long predates contact with Europeans. It supersedes any assertion or assumption of sovereignty by states such as Britain or Canada. Our land is a gift from the Creator. Our sovereignty is our birthright. Our birthright is inalienable and cannot be transferred or taken from us.

For Indigenous peoples, these are self-evident truths. As is the fact that we have the right to self-determination — which we enjoyed for tens of thousands of years before the arrival of the Europeans on our territory. We are still today entitled to freely and independently determine our own political, legal, economic, social and cultural systems without external interference. As Indigenous peoples, we have the right to make decisions about our political status and development according to our own beliefs, world views, priorities, traditions and aspirations for the future. We possess the inherent power to govern our territories and ourselves and international law recognizes that we have the collective right to self-determination. As Indigenous peoples, our political status is equal to all other peoples in the world.

We will fight to ensure that Canada respects those principles. What we are seeking is a remaking of Canada on those principles in the same way that the Indigenous president of Bolivia, Evo Morales, is working toward what he calls the "refounding" of his country as a "plurinational state," a collection of Indigenous and non-Indigenous peoples that function with respect for one another and for Mother Earth. Ecuador has come to a similar understanding with the Indigenous peoples within its borders, recognizing the equality of Indigenous nations with the larger state.

This road is open to Canada as well, and it can lead to a better world for all. I call on the Canadian people to walk this road with us.

I call on the Canadian people because in all honesty, I do not see any reason to have hope in this government or from those Indigenous organizations who are paid to echo the government's words and to deliver their programs and services to our impoverished people.

Before the last election, I know some Indigenous peoples listened to Justin Trudeau's soothing words, his seemingly heartfelt promises, and they were touched when they saw the tears in his eye and heard the catch in his throat when he spoke about the injustices done to us in the past. Some believed him when he said Canada would change, really change, and would take our hand and walk into a common future with us. Justin, like a young suitor, said he would respect our wishes, would respect our boundaries and respect our values and make amends for all of the wrongs done to us. They believed him because he told us he would adopt all ninety-four action items of the Truth and Reconciliation Report and would officially adopt the UN Declaration of the Rights of Indigenous Peoples into Canadian law.

Then slowly, blow by blow, he broke the heart of the believers by breaking his promises. The first was UNDRIP. We were shocked when he used one of our own, Jody Wilson-Raybould, to tell us that UNDRIP would not be implemented except in some kind of toothless Canadian version that they would cook up in the Indigenous and Northern Affairs and Department of Justice's backrooms. Then we heard that his promises to protect the earth were worthless as well, when his environment minister stated that, in fact, Stephen Harper's greenhouse gas targets, which she had previously ridiculed as too little too late, would now become the Trudeau government's targets.

It didn't stop there. Almost ten years of climate deniers in the Harper government were replaced by the Trudeau climate liars. While claiming to be environmentalists, this government is, in its actions, virtually identical to the Harper government. Just in my region alone, it has given a permit for the Site C dam, which will flood many square kilometres of Aboriginal title lands without the free prior and informed consent of the peoples involved — something that was promised us from both UNDRIP and the TRC. Then he approved the Pacific NorthWest LNG project, which would produce more than five million tonnes of carbon dioxide a year and threaten Indigenous coastal and interior lands. Finally, Trudeau announced that he would ram the Kinder Morgan pipeline through from the dirty tar sands to the B.C. coast, passing through more than five hundred kilometres of our Secwepemc land, and his minister warned us that the military would be used against us if we resisted. His government has crossed the line — a line that even our abuser Stephen Harper had dared not cross. It has shown that it not only did not care for us, it holds us in something that almost seems like contempt. How else can we describe these betrayals?

CHAPTER 42
BACK TO THE FUTURE

Sadly, the government's refusal to listen to our people is not the result of ignorance on their part, which could be cured by educating them about what needs to be done. The truth is, the government knows exactly what needs to be done and they have known this for at least thirty years. I know this is the case, because the government itself has had the path laid out for it several times by its own studies and commissions, as well as by the Supreme Court and by international organizations. It has simply refused, point blank, to deviate from what is essentially its oppressive, colonialist track.

The first comprehensive study of how the Indigenous right to self-determination could be accommodated within the Canadian space was actually commissioned by Justin's father. In 1983, Pierre Trudeau put Liberal MP and academic Keith Penner in charge of the Indian Affairs Self-Government Committee in the House of Commons. His report, generally referred to as the Penner Report, was the first serious rethinking of the relationship between Indigenous and non-Indigenous people in Canada. It begins with a telling quote from Leo Tolstoy:

I sit on a man's back choking him and making
him carry me and yet assure myself and others
that I am sorry for him and wish to lighten
his load by all possible means — except by
getting off his back.

For the next two hundred pages, Penner went on to describe how the government of Canada could, in important ways, get off the back of Indigenous peoples. This is an outline of how they saw the new relationship:

1. Recognition of Indian First Nation
governments with powers and jurisdiction
appropriate to a distinct order of government
within the Canadian Federation;

2. Fiscal arrangements suited to self-
governing entities;

3. A secure economic base, including land,
water and resource rights, which, together
with educational and community services
appropriate to modern society would
strengthen the culture and economy of
First Nations;

4. Economic settlement of claims to restore
capital trust accounts resources and lands to
the First Nations.

Admittedly, this first attempt was vague in some areas, but it was clear that "Indian bands" should have a greatly expanded land base — one that would allow them to build a viable economic base for their nation — and they should have sole control of and the power to make laws about the use of lands and resources. The report also made it clear that all Indian territories were to be exempt from provincial regulations and control and, in fact, that the Indigenous governing structures be equivalent to the provinces, with their own constitutionally mandated powers. Indian government would exercise its power jointly with provincial or federal governments on lands subject to Indian rights that are not reserved for Indians — that is, in treaty land claims areas. Within each subject area, an Indian government would exercise powers over all people inside its territorial limits. Non-members moving onto Indian lands to live, do business or visit would be governed by the laws of the Indian nation.

There was a brief flare-up of hope when the report was tabled in the House of Commons in March 1984, but a few months later there was a change of leadership in the Liberal party and the new leader, John Turner, ignored the plan. Then in the fall of 1984, the Liberals were swept out of power by the Mulroney Progressive Conservatives and the Penner Report was tossed aside.

We do not know for certain what the Liberals would actually have done with the Penner Report if they remained in office, but we do know what they did after 1993 when the Chrétien government came to power and, in a move repeated by Justin Trudeau twenty years later, immediately ditched the progressive measures for Indigenous peoples that they had been elected on.

In 1996, the Chrétien government was presented with the massive Royal Commission on Aboriginal Peoples

(RCAP) Report that had been commissioned by the Mulroney government in the wake of the Oka uprising. But as soon as it arrived on their doorstep, the Chrétien government dismissed all four volumes and more than fifteen hundred pages and more than four hundred recommendations by saying: No worry, we are already doing those things.

Twenty years later, the government response to the Truth and Reconciliation Report, which was published in summary form only months before the election of the Trudeau government, has been at times more nuanced but the end result has been the same. They have been doing a cynical dance around the substantial elements while they pick the low-hanging fruits that fit into their programs and services dependency basket.

In content, both the RCAP Report and the Truth and Reconciliation Report are remarkably similar and they cover substantially the same territory as the Penner Report, but with a deeper analysis.

Canada's colonial and at times genocidal behaviour toward Indigenous peoples was well-documented in the RCAP Report and many of its central points found their way into the Truth and Reconciliation Commission (TRC) Report.

Even though the TRC Report focuses primarily on the residential school system, it gave a detailed account of the history and current state of relations between Canada and Indigenous peoples. It found acts of genocide in Canada's policies of removal of Indigenous children from their homes and forcing them into residential schools. The TRC Report stated that:

> The Canadian government pursued this policy
> of cultural genocide because it wished to divest
> itself of its legal and financial obligations to
> Aboriginal people and gain control over their
> land and resources. If every Aboriginal person
> had been absorbed into the body politic, there
> would be no reserves, no Treaties, and no
> Aboriginal rights.

In unravelling the Canadian story, both the TRC and the RCAP reports began at the beginning. RCAP had asked that the government "acknowledge that concepts such as terra nullius and the doctrine of discovery are factually, legally and morally wrong" and to declare that they would "no longer form part of law making or policy development by Canadian governments; and declaring that such concepts will not be the basis of arguments presented to the courts ..." To counter the racism of these doctrines, the Canadian government was asked to make "a declaration to these ends in the new Royal Proclamation and its companion legislation. So that the appropriate place of Aboriginal peoples in Canadian history be recognized."

The TRC picked up on this demand by calling "upon the Government of Canada, on behalf of all Canadians, to jointly develop with Aboriginal peoples a new Royal Proclamation of Reconciliation to be issued by the Crown." The proclamation would build on the Royal Proclamation of 1763 and the Treaty of Niagara of 1764, and reaffirm the nation to nation relationship between Aboriginal peoples and the Crown. The proclamation would include the repudiation of the doctrine of discovery and *terra nullius* and it would reconcile Aboriginal and Crown constitutional and legal orders to ensure that Aboriginal peoples are full partners in

Confederation, including the recognition and integration of Indigenous laws and legal traditions in negotiations and implementation processes involving treaties, land claims and other constructive agreements.

Crucially, the TRC Report demanded the full implementation of the United Nations Declaration on the Rights of Indigenous Peoples as the framework for reconciliation. When these TRC action items were made at a large public event at the release of the report, the recommendation calling on Canada to implement UNDRIP received a standing ovation by the many Canadian representatives, politicians and the public present. The one person who did not stand was the Harper government's Minister of Aboriginal Affairs and Northern Development Bernard Valcourt, and he was widely criticized by the Liberals for not embracing the report and that recommendation. But now the Liberals have largely turned their back on UNDRIP. And they are publicly pulling away from their commitment to implement any of the substantial recommendations of the TRC.

Thirty-five years after the Penner Report, and more than twenty years after the RCAP, and now two years after the TRC, the federal government remains on our back, choking us while they assure themselves that, as in the Tolstoy image, they are sorry for us and wish to lighten our load "by all possible means" — except by getting off our back.

Our children continue to strain under their weight, and another generation heads to the barricades.

CHAPTER 43

THE SIX-STEP PROGRAM TO DECOLONIZATION

Hope, for me, comes from both the Indigenous youth from across the country who are ready to fight for our rights and from the non-Indigenous who I meet in university lecture halls and church basements who are not only open to re-envisioning Canada, but are willing to stand shoulder to shoulder with us in remaking it. That is our new starting point.

Travelling along the path toward decolonization will take courage for Canadians. But once you begin, I think you will find the route is not complicated and the only guide you will need is a sense of justice and decency. No need to go through the thousands of pages of government commissioned reports and many thousands more of court judgements setting out our rights, and the scores of UN reports describing Canada as a human rights abuser, to find your way. In fact, I will make it easy for you. Below is a six-point map of the path to decolonization that Canada's own experts have already laid out:

1. The first step is a simple one and has been advocated by both the RCAP and the TRC: Formally denounce the racist doctrine of discovery and terra

nullius as justification for settler presence on our
lands, as well as any other doctrines, laws or policies
that would allow you to address us on any other basis
than nation to nation.

2. As part of the nation to nation negotiation you must,
logically, recognize our right to self-determination,
which is the essential decolonizing remedy to move
Indigenous peoples from dependency to freedom.

3. Acknowledgement of our right to self-determination
must be according to international human rights
standards and include ecological and equitable
development principles, Indigenous knowledge systems,
laws, relationships to land, world views, technologies,
innovations and practices and, of course, recognition
and affirmation of our Aboriginal title and rights to the
lands that the Creator has given each nation and which
we have inhabited since time immemorial.

4. At this point we can finally sit down together for
the long, grown-up talk about who we are and what
we need, and who you are and what you need, and we
can then begin to sort out the complicated questions
about access to our lands and sharing the benefits.
These talks can, indeed, lead to reconciliation, but
only after our rights as title holders and decision
makers on the land and our economic and cultural
needs are met. We in turn will ensure that your very
real human right to be here after four hundred years
is respected and your economic and cultural needs
are also met.

5. Anything that we agree to in access and benefits must also include clear jurisdictional lines of authority based on the standard of free, prior and informed consent of Indigenous peoples and decision making that incorporates environmental reviews and oversight in accordance with Indigenous laws.

6. In concrete Canadian terms, Section 35 of the Canadian Constitution must be made to comply with Article 1 of the ICCPR/ICESCR and Article 3 of UNDRIP and all of the colonial laws must be struck from Canadian books, thereby implementing the Indigenous right to freely determine our own political status and freely pursue our economic, social and cultural development.

I promise you again that this does not have to be a painful process. It can be a liberation for you as well as for us. These simple steps could transform Canada into one of the most politically and environmentally progressive countries in the world, one that could be an example for all on how the ugly past of colonialism and racism, that has been so catastrophic for our people in terms of the sheer brutality we have been subject to, can finally be laid to rest. And both Indigenous peoples and Canadians can finally turn away from that sad past and look to a much brighter future.

But I hope you forgive us if we also insist that, before we actually embark on this new relationship with Canada, we have a kind of internationally monitored pre-nup. (To be honest, we have had a little too much experience with the European forked tongue in general and Prime Minister Trudeau's in particular.) So we would also be calling for the establishment at the UN of an oversight mechanism for Indigenous peoples. The appropriate UN body should formulate recommendations and proposals for the development of measures and activities to 1) prevent self-determination violations by all states, including Canada, against Indigenous peoples; 2) insist any violations of the right to self-determination are immediately corrected by the states, including Canada; and 3) coordinate cooperation with other UN bodies to ensure international oversight of self-determination for Indigenous peoples and immediately report any violations to the General Assembly. At the same time, Indigenous peoples must also be given permanent observer status within the UN system to enable our voices to be directly heard within the General Assembly.

We will know that Canada is finally decolonized when Indigenous peoples are exercising our inherent political and legal powers in our own territories up to the standard recognized by the United Nations, when your government has instituted sweeping policy reform based on Indigenous rights standards and when our future generations can live in sustainable ways on an Indigenous designed and driven economy.

This cannot be done in a day but the process can be started today. One hundred and fifty years is a long time to wait for justice, and there have already been too many missed chances. In fact, I sometimes wonder where we would be if Justin Trudeau's father and my father, Pierre Trudeau and George Manuel, had sat down after the Red Paper presentation ceremony in 1970 with a resolve to break the chains of colonialism and the crushing weight of poverty it shackles Indigenous peoples with.

For Indigenous peoples, it would have meant thousands of years more life than the stunted life expectancy colonialism leaves us with. Thousands of years less imprisonment and despair than colonialism serves us with. Thousands of years more education that colonialism has denied us. It would have allowed us to free the genius of our peoples to build vibrant societies within the Canadian space.

But it is never too late to start to prevent these scourges of the past from populating our collective future. It is not necessary to pass on this legacy of misery to yet another generation. Because we must be clear: unless we fix Canada in a fundamental way, we will be leaving our children with the same bitter pill that our parents left us.

So Mr. Prime Minister, you must know that Canada's cruel legacy cannot be settled by fiddling with programs and services or by hugs and tears. We need fundamental change to fix Canada because it is Canada that is broken. Either that, or we pass on this sad legacy to our children. Mine, I know, have run out of patience. They are ready to fight it out and this is the last thing I want for them — or for your children, for that matter. So let us avoid that. Relieve your children from the international embarrassment and the moral disgrace of riding on our backs and relieve my children from the crushing burden of carrying them. If we do this right, some day they may even be able to walk freely together in friendship.

LETTERS TO FRIENDS AND ENEMIES

I have drafted a collection of open letters to those people who still hold sway over us, who are in a position to right past wrongs and to the next generation in the struggle. I have decided to write this in the form of letters because they convey the sense of immediacy and urgency that our message requires. And because letters — one dear person addressing another dear person — remind us that, in the midst of our institutions caught up in great historical forces, we must not forget that we are, at the fundamental level, part of the human family and we should act in that spirit.

1. Open Letter to Pope Francis
2. Open Letter to the Secretary-General of the United Nations
3. Open Letter to the Queen of Canada
4. Open Letter to the Chief Justice of Canada
5. Open Letter to the Defenders of the Land

OPEN LETTER TO POPE FRANCIS

I am writing you as both a man who has shown his care and compassion for the peoples of this world as well as the holder of the office that has been the cause of such prolonged and extreme misery for Indigenous peoples for more than five hundred years.

You, an Argentine, a man of this hemisphere, should be able to understand this better than most popes. I am a member of the Secwepemc Nation from the Interior of British Columbia, Canada's most western province, and we are still fighting against the bitter legacy of European colonialism that was given a legal basis by one of your predecessors, Pope Nicholas V.

Pope Nicholas V's charters gave the Church's blessing to the slave trade and legitimized genocide against what he described as pagans and Saracens — which included everyone in the world other than European Christians. This began the organized international European assault, with the goal of stripping the world of its wealth and reducing its peoples to servitude. The goal of raw theft and enslavement remained the same and they are still the ultimate legal justification for European colonialism in the Americas, as well as the ultimate constitutional basis for settler colonialism.

That is why my people, and Indigenous peoples around the world, have asked you to publicly renounce the doctrine of discovery and the papal bulls of Pope Nicholas V. You alone in the world have the power to do this and such an act would help to restore the faith of many of my people in the justice of the Church. It would also in no small measure assist us in winning justice here in Canada, because those Church doctrines remain, more than five hundred years later, the core legal justification for the confiscation of our lands and subjugation of our peoples.

It is no accident that the slave trade was launched at the same time as the first brutal attacks on Indigenous lands and peoples. The slave trade, we know, was abandoned when it ceased to be profitable in the system of production, but colonialism has remained deeply imbedded in our legal systems, allowing Europeans and their successor states to control Indigenous lands for their resource wealth. It is our task to uproot this colonialism and put it into the trash bin of history alongside the slave trade.

But first, we need your help by renouncing the terrible injustices the previous holders of your office unleashed on us. We ask you, as a man of God and a man of the Americas, to stand up and speak on behalf of the people that your church played such a devastating role in oppressing.

We are waiting for you to lift the crushing weight off our back and we serve notice to you and to the world that we no longer intend to suffer in silence.

OPEN LETTER TO THE SECRETARY-GENERAL OF THE UNITED NATIONS

First, let me welcome you as the new Secretary-General of the United Nations, on behalf of a nation that is still waiting for you to recognize us. I know you are relatively new to the job, but we have been knocking at your office door for many decades, waiting to be let in.

You are, I understand, Portuguese, so that already gives us a curious connection. It was, after all, a Portuguese king who commissioned Amerigo Vespucci in his travels to our hemisphere and, for reasons I have never understood, his first name was given to not one but two continents. (It would be like me travelling to Europe and then my people deciding to name Europe and Africa as North Arthur and South Arthur. And this was only the first of many of Europeans' bizarre namings — like calling us "Indians" . . . but that is another story.)

At any rate, you shouldn't have trouble recognizing us no matter what name you use. According to the UN's own estimates, Indigenous peoples around the world number 370 million — which would make us the third largest country in the world after China and India. And over the past century, we haven't been hiding out. Indigenous peoples were in London and Paris since the 1500s and more recently, thousands of Indigenous peoples from the European empires dutifully travelled to Europe to fight in the First World War and many gave their lives for the allied cause. We were also there after the war for the launch of the forerunner of the United Nations, the League of Nations. Then in 1923,

Deskaheh, a hereditary chief of the Cayugas, travelled to Geneva on a Haudenosaunee passport to address the League of Nations. The door was opened for him until the British imperialists moved to slam it shut. This is a little problem you have. Big powers forever beating upon the small. One law for the powerful and another for the weak, and the failure to address these issues had you once again at one another's throats in the Second World War.

The United Nations at least struggles against this. When the WWII victors were still occupying the lands of the defeated, the UN drafted the Universal Declaration of Human Rights and the International Covenant on Economic, Social and Cultural Rights, which in Article 1 states that all peoples have the right of self-determination. By virtue of that right, they freely determine their political status and freely pursue their economic, social and cultural development.

And we are peoples. The UN has recognized this with the UN Declaration of the Rights of Indigenous Peoples, which passed the General Assembly in September 2007, which also states in Article 3 that

> Indigenous peoples have the right to self-determination. By virtue of that right they freely determine their political status and freely pursue their economic, social and cultural development.

So, here we are, at your door. The third largest block of humanity asking to be let in. To refuse us is to collaborate with the crimes that have been committed against us. We demand to be heard by the society of nations in the name of justice, in the name of decency, in the name of humanity. Not only heard, but listened to.

To refuse Indigenous nations the rights promised all nations in the international covenants and UNDRIP is to break the international law you are sworn to uphold. You must insist that Canada — as well as similar settler colonial countries like the US, Australia and New Zealand — respect the international treaties they signed to respect the fundament human rights of all peoples. If you fail to do so, you are sending out the message, loud and clear, that UN treaties are not worth the paper they are written on.

But we are optimistic people. We believe in fresh starts and change for the better. We are willing to give you a chance to settle into your new job. But while you are getting used to your new surroundings, please know that we are still at the door, waiting. You should let us in sooner rather than later because we will never, ever go away. We cannot. Because as part of the family of nations, we have nowhere else to go.

OPEN LETTER TO THE QUEEN OF CANADA

First, I would like to offer you a familiar greeting. After all, your people and my people go back a long time together. Your family tree, from the House of Hanover in 1714 and the successor House of Windsor from 1901, gives you a perspective that few others have on the modern world. You personally, as inheritor of the Houses of Hanover and Windsor, have been with us, without our consent, for all those many centuries.

If you like, I can remind you of some of the highlights. Beginning with your servant, British Royal Naval Captain James Cook, who claimed my people's lands for your possession in 1778 by sailing by the Pacific coast. It doesn't matter that my people's lands are four hundred kilometres from the coast, James Cook — who was soon after executed by the Hawaiians for the same sort of nonsense — claimed all of the land to the Rocky Mountains on the weight of a sail-by of the coast. A few decades later, a few of your agents from the Crown monopoly of the Hudson Bay Company stumbled into our lands from the East and "discovered" our peoples and our rivers. Company men came later and trading posts were built in strategic places on our lands and we permitted this because the trade was useful for us. And because they were still the only representatives of the Crown on our territory, they were given a charter to run it as a business — which for them was what this new land was. For us, of course, it was and remains a homeland . . . but I am getting ahead of myself.

My people and all of the Indigenous people in this vast territory were still not aware that we had become your possession. We had never surrendered it and we never will. But your servants did not bother with such niceties. When an official colony was created, the first law they passed in their legislature was that Indians did not have the right to vote.

There is a word for this mass disenfranchisement of a racial majority by the racial minority and the seizure of the subject race's land and that word is apartheid. That is exactly what the white society in British Columbia adopted and, at different times and in different ways, what all of Canada adopted. The original apartheid is still there.

This troubling history is why we have to begin by going through our family histories and determining how, exactly, Your family decided it should be in possession of our lands. I promise you, if you can find anything that even remotely resembles a bill of sale, I will gladly acknowledge it. But we both know you will not find one because it does not exist. And after you have rummaged around the attic in your castle for it and have to admit what we both know already — that it does not exist — I ask you to act in the spirit of the Honour of the Crown that we hear so much about, and instruct your servants to come to us and acknowledge that these lands are indeed ours, and sit down with us to see if at long last we can work something out that is fair to all.

And I promise you that we will be fair. We are not strangers and we will act as good neighbours. Who knows, maybe someday we can even become friends.

We will see. But first, I am sure you will understand, we must insist that you give us back what you stole — or at least what has been stolen in your name. We believe that, as someone who claims to be a decent woman, you can do no less.

OPEN LETTER TO THE CHIEF JUSTICE OF CANADA

Let me begin with a sincere thanks. You won our respect for a statement you made in May 2015, on the eve of the publication of the Truth and Reconciliation Report, when you pointed out that Canada had been guilty of cultural genocide in its treatment of Indigenous peoples. Your statement was a clear and unvarnished description of the facts and it sent shockwaves through a country that was not familiar with hearing the truth. Let me remind you of the force of your words:

"After an initial period of inter-reliance and equality," you said, "Canada developed an 'ethos of exclusion and cultural annihilation.' The objective — I quote from Sir John A. Macdonald, our revered forefather — was to 'take the Indian out of the child,' and thus solve what was referred to as the Indian problem. 'Indianness' was not to be tolerated; rather it must be eliminated. In the buzz-word of the day, assimilation; in the language of the twenty-first century, cultural genocide."

When Indigenous peoples have accused the Canadian government of cultural genocide, they were quickly dismissed, even mocked. But your statement, repeated a short time later by the Honourable Justice Murray Sinclair and Marie Wilson and Chief Wilton Littlechild in the Truth and Reconciliation Commission Report, made Canadians, at least momentarily, face the facts. Evil had been done in their name and it was up to them to right the wrong. In this you performed a valuable service and for this we thank you.

Still, even though we are grateful for that, I would like to very respectfully point out that there remains a little work left to do in your own back yard, the Supreme Court of Canada, which as John Borrows has pointed out, has had to reach for magic crystals to justify Crown title over our lands. We ask you to set aside the colonial black magic and simply look outside the window at your court. You will see the churning rapids of the Ottawa River that have been flowing since time immemorial. The first European to lay eyes on that magnificent sight was Champlain's boy Étienne Brûlé, who the Algonquin agreed to take inland with them on a regular summer trip to Wendat country to trade their manufactures — canoes, snowshoes and baskets — for Iroquoian corn, beans and squash. The land and the river was never surrendered by the Algonquin and the French teenager from a rough Paris suburb was not in a position to make a European assertion of sovereignty. He was a passenger and a guest who was there to learn the language so he could interpret the business arrangements between the Algonquin and Champlain. The Algonquin never agreed to surrender that land. Not then and at no time in the four hundred years since have they agreed to surrender the land you see outside of your window. It was and remains Indigenous land.

We ask only that you admit this simple truth with the same courage as you admitted the truth of the genocide against our peoples. Because then and only then will we be able to sit together and fix the problem in a way that is fair to the Indigenous and non-Indigenous. Only then will the Canadian legal system become at long last, not just a legal system, but a justice system.

OPEN LETTER TO THE DEFENDERS OF THE LAND

We meet at our rare gatherings, and more often I see you again on the land — on bush road blockades where you build smoky fires to keep the mosquitos down in summer and big crackling fires in the winter to try to soften the force of the icy winds. And I see you on television newscasts and sometimes even I don't know who it is behind the mask — from which nation or even woman or man. But it doesn't matter. You are taking a stand, defending the one irreplaceable thing in the world — our land. Without it we are lost. We are nothing.

You do this in the tradition of our people, without violence. Your weapon is your body and your strong will, your refusal to surrender your spirit. You offer yourself to the forces of injustice to let them know how profoundly our spirits are offended by the theft of our land and its desecration. You stand in front of our legal authorities demanding justice. You stand in front of the world demanding justice.

What no one sees is the suffering you endure — personal poverty, uncertainty about whether your actions have meaning, whether your sacrifice is in vain and fear that when the time comes you will break and run.

But you don't run. They take you away, another takes your place. Our people owe a debt of gratitude to all of the land defenders and I offer my most sincere thanks for your leadership. You have earned a place of honour in our towns and villages and as long as you are left standing, we will never truly be conquered.

AFTERWORD

SETTLING WITH CANADA: A DEBT COMING DUE

Grand Chief Ronald Derrickson

Although we all miss him terribly, Arthur's friends and family have tried to ensure that his struggle has not missed a step. In the most immediate and visible terms, it is being carried on by his partner, Nicole, and his children.

Less than a month after Arthur's January 15, 2017, funeral, Nicole ensured that a planned meeting of Arthur's colleagues from across the country took place in Kamloops to discuss how they could continue to work together without Arthur there to direct the traffic. In April, the same thing was done to cover his work at the United Nations Permanent Forum on Indigenous Issues. Arthur had attended every meeting of the Permanent Forum since its launch in 2002. He was a longtime representative of the North American Indigenous Caucus and served as the co-chair of the Global Indigenous Caucus. At the April 2017 Forum, both his son, Ska7cis, and his daughter, Kanahus, travelled to New York in his place. They were determined that no vacuum would be left in his legacy.

In his father's place, Ska7cis made an impassioned plea with the anti-colonial message expressed in this book. His daughter, Kanahus, was not shy in confronting the Canadian Minister of Indigenous Affairs, Carolyn Bennett, on the floor of the UN after her speech, and in front of a rolling camera, to point out the parts of the minister's speech that were blatantly untrue. The work of correcting lies and advocating for our peoples continues. In the beginning of August 2017, Arthur's close friend and colleague Russell Diabo travelled to Geneva to ensure that the facts, and not Canada's distortions, were put before the world human rights body. I helped fund this trip because I believe that it is essential that we continue to inform the world of Canada's crimes.

So we are all continuing down the path he laid out for us. In my case, that means following up the work we did together on how Canada is hiding from its books the debt it owes Indigenous peoples.

I would like to take a moment to describe what we are up against in this area. Because we have been dispossessed of our land and the wealth it generates, the Indigenous movement is basically a poor people's movement, and because of that, even most of our own people do not fully understand what is owed to us. And Canada does everything it can to obscure this fact.

Today Canada shows only $890 million owed to us in the Indian trust funds, and it lists only $15.3 billion in contingent liabilities for the "land claims" they hope to settle. So the total liability they are claiming on their books for Indigenous peoples and Indigenous lands comes to roughly $16 billion.

In fact, that is a tiny fraction of what is owed. For treaty peoples, the government's own accounting shows that among the numbered treaties, the shortfall in payments and benefits from unfulfilled treaty promises amounts to $42,000 per person, which already adds up to $20 billion in unpaid benefits.

At the same time, one Alberta band alone, the Mikisew Cree, has filed a $10-billion lawsuit against the federal and Alberta governments for cheating them on treaty deals, endangering the water quality in the Peace/Athabasca river delta and for allowing energy companies to divert too much water for use in oil sands operations, disrupting hunting and trapping and causing economic losses. Multiply that $10 billion by six hundred bands, and you begin to get a glimpse of the true legal liability that Canada is facing.

Even these hundreds of billions of dollars owed Indigenous peoples are still just the low-hanging fruit. When you start adding in compensation for stolen resources, estimates of Canada's debt to Indigenous peoples quickly surpasses $2 trillion and continues to rise. Some researchers have even put the debt owed Indigenous people for the wealth extracted from our lands in the $650 trillion range. We cannot yet verify that amount, but even with a $2 trillion debt, the amount Canada spends on Indigenous people each year (the overwhelming majority of which goes to the bureaucrats) is only a tiny percentage of the interest accruing. Canada pockets the rest, year after year.

That same $2 trillion instantly doubles the Canadian debt and puts the debt-to-GDP ratio up to around 175 per cent from the current 85 per cent. If Canada honestly accounts for what it owes Indigenous peoples, it is effectively bankrupt. Among the actions we should be taking now is suing the big credit rating companies like Standard and Poor's for being complicit in hiding this debt even though they were informed of it by Arthur Manuel in his meetings with them a decade ago — and they agreed with him that it existed.

That balance is now coming due and I will be giving a more detailed breakdown of these figures over the coming months and years and we will be making them public as part of our drive to hold Canada accountable on the balance sheet.

We are all, in fact, continuing the work Arthur started. We are part of a political legacy that also included George Manuel and Bobby Manuel and that now includes a whole generation who are no longer willing to accept living, as Arthur pointed out, on 0.2 per cent of our land while our territories are stripped of their wealth and our waters poisoned. Our numbers increase with our outrage over the theft of our land, our resources and the ongoing attempt to steal our future. You will be hearing from us.

APPENDIX

The following article completed by Arthur Manuel less than two weeks before his death, on December 31, 2016, was not part of the original manuscript. It was published in the *First Nations Strategic Bulletin* and it was Arthur's look ahead to Canada's 150th anniversary year.

"ARE YOU A CANADIAN?"

The 150th anniversary of the *BNA Act*, where our lands were officially stolen from underneath us, is a time to protest, but it is also a time for reflection. This is an important milestone and it is time for us to decide if we want to continue to be colonized peoples or if we want to seek self-determination.

We have to face the fact that Canada is a settler state that was created by Great Britain to take over our Indigenous territories for use and benefit of Canada. This kind of human exploitation is called colonization and it is designed to give settler Canadians ownership over all Indigenous lands. Indigenous peoples basically subsidize the Canadian economy with free land.

Colonization is a complex relationship but simple to understand if you know that dispossession, dependency and oppression are the consequences that it is designed to produce between the colonizer and the colonized. It is important to understand the United Nations (UN) has condemned colonization in all its manifestations because the moment you dispossess someone of their land and make him or her dependent upon the colonizer, you create a person willing to fight to be free and independent again. In this way, colonialism is against world peace.

Canadian colonialism is also based on racial discrimination, which is deeply engrained in the entire constitutional and legal fabric of Canada. Indigenous peoples need to be careful not to honour the 150 years of colonization because this will validate the racism that is implicit in Canadian colonialism. Instead, Indigenous peoples and Canadians who believe in human rights need look at Canada's 150th Birthday Party as a period to undertake a commitment to decolonize Canada and recognize the right of Indigenous peoples to self-determination.

In practical terms we need to look first at the results of colonial dispossession: the minuscule land base that Indigenous peoples have in contrast to settler Canadians. Our Indian reserves are only 0.2 per cent of Canada's land mass yet Indigenous peoples are expected to survive on that land base. This has led to the systematic impoverishment of Indigenous peoples and this impoverishment is a big part of the crippling oppression Indigenous peoples suffer under the existing Canadian colonial system.

This 0.2 per cent systemic impoverishment is used as a weapon by Canada to keep us too poor and weak to fight back. It is used to bribe and co-opt Indigenous leadership into becoming neocolonial partners to treat the symptoms of poverty on the Indian reserve without addressing the root cause of the problem, which is the dispossession of all of the Indigenous peoples' territory by Canada and the provinces.

Settler Canadians, on the other hand, enjoy and benefit from 99.8 per cent of our Indigenous land base under the federal and provincial governments. That is what the first Canadian Constitution established under the *British North America Act 1867*. Our lands were put under Crown title and we were left with 0.2 per cent of the land on our Indian reserves. Indigenous peoples living on "Indian reserves" do NOT get equal programs and services that settler Canadians get. There has always been a battle between the federal and provincial governments about what order of government is responsible for programs and services on Indian reserves. Even in these practical terms we seem to belong to neither, and the question again is: are Indigenous peoples Canadians?

Does this make us Canadians when programs and services are NOT available to us when we live on our Indian reserves? Indeed 50 per cent of Indian people live off their Indian reserves because of the lack of land, employment and education opportunities on our existing Indian reserves. Indigenous peoples only become Canadians by migrating to Canada based on need and not because they want to. These 0.2 per cent Indian reserves are in constant turmoil with their colonial masters and this is really spelled out in the Royal Commission on Aboriginal Peoples Report 1996.

The United Nations human rights bodies under the human rights treaties like the International Covenant on Civil and Political Rights, International Covenant on Economic Social and Cultural Rights and International Convention on the Elimination of All Forms of Racial Discrimination have made many human rights recommendations to Canada. Canada has ignored these human rights recommendations because Canada's existing policy is to terminate Indigenous constitutional and legal rights and assimilate Indigenous peoples into Canada as a settler state.

I was an elected 0.2 per cent chief of my reserve for eight years. I found out very early how futile it is to tinker with programs and services within the 0.2 per cent land base. Canada and the provinces have never seriously wanted to increase the land base of Indigenous peoples in Canada and Indigenous peoples have always had to depend on the Supreme Court of Canada to put pressure on the government to address the land issues of Indigenous peoples. Nevertheless, the SCC also has only found Tsilhqot'in people had Aboriginal title over 1,750 square kilometers in the Tsilhqot'in Case of 2014.

Everyone needs to take into consideration that Canada is the second largest country in the world with a population of thirty-five million people of which one million are Indigenous. British Columbia is as large as California, Oregon and Washington States combined, which have a population of more than forty million people, and has a population of only 4.6 million people of which 200,000 are Indigenous people. In Canada the size, population, constitutional and legal framework could accommodate fundamental change in expanding the land base of Indigenous peoples from 0.2 per cent to a size that could accommodate our right to self-determination.

The new land base has to be based on the human rights of Indigenous peoples to enjoy self-determination as Indigenous nations. These land bases need to be large enough to protect our languages, cultures, laws and economies. Canadians must accept that the existing 0.2 per cent model does not work. That fundamental increase must be made to accommodate

Aboriginal and Treaty rights to land. These ultimately larger land bases will be part of Canada's economy. It will provide Indigenous peoples with the right to influence economic development choices because of our increased governance over our larger land base.

These are the broad fundamental arrangements that the Supreme Court of Canada is dealing with when making decisions regarding Aboriginal and treaty rights cases. The Supreme Court of Canada takes a broader view of these rights and it is up to the executive branches of Canada and the provinces to manifest these legal directions in terms of consistent policies on Canada's Constitution and land rights of Indigenous peoples which were set out in section 35(1) in Canada's Constitution 1982.

These broader issues are going to manifest themselves in the struggle of Indigenous peoples to find land settlements in British Columbia and to come to some decision regarding climate change and the Kinder Morgan Trans Mountain Pipeline Expansion project. Canada's existing Indigenous land policies have been a failure in British Columbia and across the country. It is apparent that the Justin Trudeau government is trying to circumvent dealing with the 0.2 per cent problem by giving more money for programs and services. This may help our Band Administrations to bandage up the 0.2 per cent system but it will not address the root cause of the poverty the 0.2 per cent system generates day-after-day in our families.

Every Indigenous nation in British Columbia should be recognized to have exclusive rights regarding a land base of 3–5 million acres of land and water base to protect our language, culture, laws and economy. The United States was much more open in giving tribes larger land bases than

Canada. The large reserves in the USA provide a greater economic independence for the tribes, but they are still part of the US economies. Canadians need to realize that we must embark on a new direction after 150 years of colonization of Indigenous peoples. It must be a system based on the international human rights of Indigenous peoples as nations.

I believe that under the existing colonial system in Canada, Indigenous peoples are not Canadian because of the systemic impoverishment we are forced live in because we are alienated from our traditional territories. If we accept colonization as a foundation of our relationship to Canada, we are endorsing our own impoverishment. You cannot have reconciliation under the colonial 0.2 per cent Indian reserve system. It is impossible. Nothing can justify that kind of human degradation. The land issue must be addressed before reconciliation can begin.

ABOUT THE AUTHORS

Photo by Nicole Schabus

ARTHUR MANUEL was a widely respected Indigenous leader and activist from the Secwepemc Nation. He entered the world of Indigenous politics in the 1970s, as president of the Native Youth Association. He went on to serve as chief of the Neskonlith Indian Band near Chase, B.C., and elected chair of the Shuswap Nation Tribal Council. He was also active in the Assembly of First Nations and a spokesperson for Defenders of the Land, an organization dedicated to environmental justice. Manuel is the co-author of *Unsettling Canada: A National Wake Up Call*, with Grand Chief Ronald Derrickson. This book won the 2016 Canadian Historical Association Best Book Prize. He was known internationally, having advocated for Indigenous rights and struggles at the United Nations, The Hague and the World Trade Organization.

Photo by West Kelowna Photography

GRAND CHIEF RONALD DERRICKSON served as Chief of the Westbank First Nation from 1976 to 1986 and from 1998 to 2000. He was made Grand Chief by the Union of B.C. Indian Chiefs in 2012. Grand Chief Derrickson is one of the most successful Indigenous business owners in Canada.

INDEX

A

Aboriginal rights. *See* Aboriginal title and rights

Aboriginal Title Alliance, 164

Aboriginal title and rights. *See also* land and resource rights for Indigenous peoples

and court injunctions, 218-219, 221-223

and economic uncertainty, 122-129, 204-209

and natural resource extraction, 19-24, 181, 186-190

and Reconciliation Framework Agreements, 204-209

and rightful title holders, 118-120, 182, 238-239, 251, 254-256

and the *Constitution Act of 1982*, 96-99

and the 1969 White Paper, 94-95

extinguishment of, 101-109, 114-117, 141, 180-181, 208

legal basis of, 88-93, 102-104, 109-112, 180-181

legal decisions affecting, 100-112

surrender of, 104-106, 120, 182, 251-252

termination of, 94-95, 153-154

activism and resistance, 18-25, 72, 84-85, 121, 124-125, 177, 213-241, 253-262. *See also* grassroots movements

Alfred, Taiaiake, 201

apartheid, 65, 153-154, 161, 287

Assembly of First Nations (AFN), 51-52, 132-133, 136, 140, 142-146, 189

assimilation, 83, 124

Atleo, Shawn, 133

B

band councils and governance, 118-120, 134-136, 182, 254-255

Bellegarde, Perry, 52, 56

Bennett, Carolyn, 49, 196, 198, 294

Billy, Janice, 84-85, 164

Borrows, John, 90-92, 110

British Columbia Treaty Process, 101, 114-117, 127, 181, 204-205

British North America Act of 1867, 61-63, 65-66, 95-99, 165-166. *See also Constitution Act of 1982*

Brûlé, Étienne, 290

C

Calder decision, 101

Canada (AG) v Lavell, 176-177

Canada-United States softwood lumber dispute, 186-189

Cardinal, Harold, 95

Carr, Jim, 55

Chief Neskonlith, 261

Chrétien, Jean, 95, 271-272

Clark, Christy, 236

colonialism. *See also* neocolonialism
> and condemnation by the
> United Nations, 168-172
> and economic dependency, 71
> and human suffering, 71, 278-
> 279, 281-282
> and racism, 76-81
> and violence, 72-74, 168
> as the foundation of Canada,
> 58-66, 212-213

Columbus, Christopher, 59

Comprehensive Land Claims
> Policy, 101-102, 104-108,
> 114-117, 204-205

*Constitution Act of 1867. See British
> North America Act of 1867*

Constitution Act of 1982, 95-99, 101,
> 116, 122, 138, 165-166, 277.
> *See also British North America
> Act of 1867*

Constitution Express, 96, 116, 125

Cook, James, 286

criminalization of Indigenous peo-
> ple, 79, 83-85, 161, 181-182,
> 215-223, 225-227, 259-260

D

Dakota Access pipeline protests,
> 253-258

Day, Ryan, 135

decolonization, 97-98, 146, 152-
> 158, 161-164, 171-172,
> 275-279

Defenders of the Land, 24-25, 28,
> 151-152, 155, 161, 224-225,
> 227, 291

Delgamuukw v British Columbia
> (1997), 19, 102, 140-141, 186

Department of Indian Affairs. *See
> Indigenous and Northern Af-
> fairs Canada*

dependency. *See economic depen-
> dency*

Derrickson, Ronald, 186

Deskaheh, 191, 283-284

Diabo, Russell, 142-143, 145-146,
> 200, 226, 294

Discovery doctrine, 89, 92-93, 273,
> 275-276

duty to consult, 102, 149, 205, 207

E

economic debt to Indigenous
> peoples, 294-296

economic dependency, 67-72,
> 136-137, 145, 147-148, 151,
> 153-154, 261-262

economy based on Indigenous
> values, 208, 243-249

Elsipogtog anti-fracking protest,
> 213, 254

environmental issues, 220-222,
> 235-249

Eyford Report, 112, 114-116

F

First Nations Summit, 136

Fontaine, Phil, 132-133

food sovereignty, 67-70, 239-240,
> 261-262

fourth world, 162, 156

Fourth World, The, 67, 85

free, prior and informed consent

    and decolonization, 277

    and Sun Peaks Resort, 164

    and the Kinder Morgan Trans Mountain Pipeline, 238, 241

    in the United Nations Declaration of the Rights of Indigenous Peoples, 53-54, 183, 193, 197, 248

fur trade, 59-60

G

genocide

    as separation from the land, 115, 117

    by residential schools, 48, 272-273, 289

    of Beothuk people, 59, 77

George, Dudley, 184

grassroots movements, 136-137, 151-158, 224-225, 227-228. *See also* activism and resistance

Gustafsen Lake stand-off, 259-260

Guterres, António, 283-285

H

Haida Nation v British Columbia (Minister of Forests), 102

Harper, Stephen, 51, 62, 81, 160, 243-244, 267-268

Horne, Matt, 236

Humphrey, John, 168

I

Idle No More, 25, 28, 136, 151-152, 155-156, 224-225, 227

Ignace, William Jones. *See* Wolverine

Imperial Metals, 220-221

incarceration of Indigenous people, 79, 181-182, 217, 225, 260

Indian Act

    adoption of, 64-65

    and governance, 118-120

    and Indian status, 177

    and restriction on land rights organizing, 240, 256

    racism and white supremacy in, 64-65

Indigenous activism and resistance. *See* activism and resistance

Indigenous and Northern Affairs Canada, 72, 134-136, 138-139, 147, 153, 200-201

Indigenous economy. *See* economy based on Indigenous values

Indigenous Network on Economies and Trade (INET), 23-24, 128, 185-186, 188-189, 237-241

Indigenous sovereignty. *See* self-determination of Indigenous peoples

Interior Alliance of B.C. Indigenous Nations, 19, 22-23, 186, 188-189

International Covenant on Civil and Political Rights (ICCPR), 144, 166, 169-170, 174, 177, 277

International Covenant on Economic, Social and Cultural Rights (ICESCR), 144, 174, 277

International Convention on the Elimination of All Forms of Racial Discrimination, 174 international economic rights advocacy, 184-190

international human rights advocacy, 96, 160-183, 293-294

Ipperwash Crisis, 183-184

J

Jackson, Andrew, 232

James Bay and Northern Quebec Agreement, 101, 107-108

John, Ed, 189

K

Keystone Pipeline, 254, 257

Kinder Morgan Trans Mountain Pipeline, 237-241, 254-258,

King, Martin Luther, Jr., 230, 255

Klein, Naomi, 254

Kyoto Protocol, 50-51

L

Lamer, Antonio, 102

land and resource rights for Indigenous peoples, 54, 98, 172, 179-181, 185-190, 193-194, 270-271, 276-277. *See also* Aboriginal title and rights

land dispossession, 60, 63, 65, 67-71, 73, 88-93

land ownership and control by Canada, 69, 63, 80-81, 88-93, 110-112, 121-124, 204-209, 276

land protection, 72, 84-85, 213-225, 238-241, 253-260

Lavell, Jeannette Corbiere, 176-177

Linden, Sidney B., 184

Lovelace, Sandra, 177

M

Mandela, Nelson, 153-154

Manuel, Anita Rose (Snutetkwe), 85

Manuel, Bobby, 155-156, 163

Manuel, George, 16-17, 67, 94-96, 139, 162-163, 202

Manuel, Mandy (Kanahus), 85, 293-294

Manuel, Nikki (Mayuk), 85

Manuel, Ska7cis, 85, 164, 293

Marshall, John, 90, 92

Mathias, Joe, 155

McKenna, Catherine, 236

McLachlin, Beverley, 48, 289-290

McNee, John, 196-198, 232

Mercredi, Ovide, 133

mining, 220-222

missing and murdered Indigenous women, 77

modified rights model, 104-105

Morales, Evo, 266

Mulroney, Brian, 114, 271-272

N

National Commission for Truth and Reconciliation Report, 48-50, 272-274, 289

National Indian Brotherhood, 95

Native Youth of Canada, 18

Nault, Robert, 140-141

neocolonialism, 132-136, 255-256. *See also* colonialism

Nisga'a Final Agreement, 103

Nkrumah, Kwame, 133

North American Free Trade Agreement (NAFTA), 186-190

O

Oregon Treaty, 90

P

Pacific NorthWest liquefied natural gas project, 236-237

Parentucelli, Tommaso. *See* Pope Nicholas V

Parrish, William, 163

Pasternak, Shiri, 218

Penner, Keith, 269-271

Penner Report, 269-272

Phillip, Stewart, 237

pipelines, 235-241, 245-246, 253-258

police violence, 72-73, 84-85, 107-108, 183-184, 215-217, 259-260

Pope Francis, 281-282

Pope Nicholas V, 58-59, 63, 281

poverty, 70-71, 78-80, 124, 136-137, 142-145, 148, 173, 278-279

Project SITKA, 226-227

prior and informed consent. *See* free, prior and informed consent

prison. *See* incarceration of Indigenous people

Q

Queen Elizabeth II, 286-288

R

racism and white supremacy
    and land entitlement, 93, 110-112, 273, 275-276

as a tool of colonialism, 76-81
    of the Canadian state, 62-66
reconciliation, 56-57, 98-99, 200-209

Reconciliation Framework Agreements (RFA), 201, 203-209

Red Chris Mine, 220-221

reserve lands, 67-68, 82-85, 180

residential schools, 48-49, 272-273, 289

resistance. *See* activism and resistance

resource extraction, 19-24, 60, 121-125, 135, 181, 220-222

resource revenue sharing, 190

resource rights. *See* land and resource rights for Indigenous peoples

Roosevelt, Eleanor, 168

Royal Commission on Aboriginal Peoples (RCAP), 49, 271-273

S

Schabus, Nicole, 24, 293

secession of Indigenous peoples from Canada, 162, 172, 194-195

Secwepemc people
    activism and resistance of, 83-85, 139, 216-217, 220-223, 237-241, 254-260
    and international human rights advocacy, 163-164, 180-182
    and reconciliation agreements, 207-208
    and food sovereignty, 261-262

Secwepemc Trans-mountain Oversight Plenary (STOP), 239

self-determination of Indigenous peoples

and decolonization, 98-99, 143-146, 152, 162, 228, 231, 265-266, 276

and international human rights treaties, 54, 166, 169-173, 178-179, 193-197

and the Eyford Report, 116

and the Penner Report, 269-271

self-government, 71, 98, 115-116, 120, 145, 166, 202, 208, 269-271

Seventh Generation Fund for Indigenous Peoples, 24, 253

Shuswap Nation Tribal Council, 18-19, 22-23, 163

Skwelkwek'welt. *See* Sun Peaks Resort

softwood lumber dispute. *See* Canada–United States softwood lumber dispute

sovereignty. *See* self-determination of Indigenous peoples

Standing Rock. *See* Dakota Access pipeline protests

Stavenhagen, Rodolfo, 164

suicide, 71, 79, 212

Sun Peaks Resort, 83-85, 164, 216-217

surveillance of Indigenous activists, 226-227, 229, 233-234

T

terra nullius doctrine, 89, 92, 273, 275-276

Thomas, Mary, 261

traditional Indigenous governance, 118-120, 139-140

Trail of Tears, 232

treaties in Canada, 90, 92, 64, 101, 122. *See also* British Columbia Treaty Process and treaty negotiations

treaty negotiations, 114-115, 141, 150-151, 204-205

Trudeau, Justin, 222-223

and environmental policy, 236-244, 266-268

and the National Commission for Truth and Reconciliation Report, 49-55

and the United Nations, 160

and the United Nations Declaration of the Rights of Indigenous Peoples, 53-55, 196-198, 225, 266-267

Trudeau, Pierre, 52, 94-95, 269

Trump, Donald, 188, 257-258

Truth and Reconciliation Report. *See* National Commission for Truth and Reconciliation Report

Tsilhqot'in Nation v. British Columbia, 109-112, 116, 127-128, 188

Turner, John, 271

U

Union of B.C. Indian Chiefs, 95-96, 155-156

United Nations

and Aboriginal title, 104

and colonialism, 74, 168-173

and international human

rights advocacy, 160-184, 283-285, 293-294

and oversight mechanism for Indigenous peoples, 277-278

and patriation of the Constitution, 165

Arthur Manuel's work with, 24

Declaration of the Rights of Indigenous Peoples, 49-55, 98, 158, 166, 170, 174, 191-198, 274, 277

Human Development Index, 78

International Covenant on Civil and Political Rights (ICCPR), 144, 166, 169-170, 174, 177, 277

International Covenant on Economic, Social and Cultural Rights (ICESCR), 144, 174, 277

United Nations Declaration of the Rights of Indigenous Peoples (UNDRIP), 49-55, 98, 158, 166, 170, 174, 191-198, 274, 277

United Nations Human Development Index, 78

Universal Declaration of Human Rights, 168-169

Unsettling Canada: A National Wake-up Call, 18, 25-26, 28-29, 94

V

Valcourt, Bernard, 274

violence

against Indigenous women, 77, 107-108, 193-194

by the Canadian state, 72-74, 84-85, 107-108, 161, 184-184, 193, 213, 215-217, 229-230, 259-260

during European colonization of Canada, 59

in activism and resistance, 229-234

W

Warriors, 233

Water Protectors. *See* Dakota Access pipeline protests

Watts, George, 155

welfare, 68-71, 78, 136, 261-262

White Paper (Statement of the Government of Canada on Indian Policy 1969), 52, 94-95, 153

white supremacy. *See* racism and white supremacy

Wilson, Bill, 155

Wilson, Judy, 135, 189, 237

Wilson-Raybould, Jody, 55, 112, 197-198

Wolverine, 67, 259-262

World Council of Indigenous Peoples, 16, 163

World Trade Organization (WTO), 186-190

Y

youth, 79, 136, 233, 275

Z

Zirnhelt, David, 22-23